Passion for Real Estate Investing

The Making of a Strategic Real Estate Investor

How you can master the markets to live the life you were designed for…

Fuquan Bilal

Dedication

This book is dedicated to my mother. Thank you, Mom for the many conversations we've had about living our best lives and adding value to others. Thanks for instilling the hustler spirit in me and teaching me how to make ambition and aspirations line up together.

Hustlers don't make excuses when they don't achieve their goals – they look at the issue square in the eye and accept it as a challenge and an opportunity to improve.

Thank you!!!

Foreword

Dr. David Phelps

The opposite of strategy is random activity. In his latest book, "Passion for Real Estate Investing," author Fuquan Bilal makes the assertion that to live out one's life dreams and goals, there must be a strategy.

Wisdom vs. knowledge. There's a difference. Knowledge is information. Wisdom is the understanding and application of that knowledge. This book is a treatise on wisdom.

From flipping and renting houses to a real estate fund manager, the author lays out his version of the entrepreneur's journey. He vividly describes not only his successes but also his failures and most importantly, the lessons he derived from those setbacks.

At first, it was trial and error accompanied by finding the right mentors. Serving first while gaining experience is one of the keys that accelerated the entrepreneurial journey for the author. The pages in the book provide an inner reflection of a passionate man who learned to be a great leader with purpose and vision.

Nothing happens without intention. Intention becomes the roadmap. The roadmap elucidates clear destination points. From there a strategy is built. No random activities but a relentless desire to improve through rapid implementation combined with learning – this is where wisdom is derived.

Not only does Fuquan have the experience and track record to speak with authority on this subject, but he also oozes with character. Knowing a man's heart, his core guiding principles and his values communicates more than knowledge...it imparts passion.

Fuquan is self-made and self-motivated. He is inquisitive and embraces both change and hard work. He does not live a life defined by others. He loves collaboration and focuses on continually improving through his personal development.

"A Passion for Real Estate Investing" is a must-read for any real estate investor-entrepreneur. It will inspire you and provide you with confidence for being your best as you pursue your path of the entrepreneur's journey to fulfill your dreams and goals.

Dr. David Phelps
Founder and CEO of Freedom Founders Mastermind
www.FreedomFounders.com

Acknowledgments

Thank You To:

Tim Houghten, who sat with me for hours asking me questions and helping me craft and polish the manuscript.

Adam Santiago, my social media manager, who helped with the book cover and marketing for the launch of the book.

LaKenya Kopf, my executive assistant who helps me with everything.

Maria Garcia, for taking the time to edit all of my books.

Passion for Real Estate Investing

The Making of a Strategic Real Estate Investor

How you can master the markets to live the life you were designed for...

Becoming a Strategic Investor

Becoming a strategic investor is the key to achieving sustainable, outsized success, and outliving the current status quo. As a strategist, you will gain better clarity on what you want, are capable of, and how to get there by making the right investments.

As a strategic investor, you will become the master of your own destiny and legacy. You'll be able to navigate on and off-road, survive economic shifts and trends, be able to balance data with human wisdom, and master your time. So, not only will you be able to achieve more, but enjoy the journey more as well.

Through better awareness, asking the right questions, and cultivating superior thinking habits, you can become a strategic investor, and master investing to get more of what you want. Keep reading to find out how...

About the Author

Passion for Real Estate Investments is the third book by Fuquan Bilal. His first two works Turning Distress into Success, and The Tire Kicker both have 5 star reviews on Amazon. Today, Fuquan heads up a multi-million dollar alternative investment fund and fathers two budding entrepreneurs.

About this Book

This book is designed to not only share my journey but to show you how I was able to make multiple leaps in investing where many get stuck. This will empower you to boost your own strategic thinking and investment acumen to achieve sustainable financial success.

It takes you from wherever you are on your journey in life and finances, to thinking like a veteran investor, who has gleaned the wisdom of working through multiple economic cycles, to finding your state of bliss and achieving living in your zone. It's about mastering money to fulfill your purpose and live out your life at its maximum capacity.

Inside these pages you'll learn to think larger and longer, to invest intelligently, like a 1%er, and to recognize how you can use your investments to impact and design your environment.

Table of Contents

- The Reality
- What Makes a Profitable Flip
- Smarter Ways to Participate
- Rental Property Investing

- The Problem with [Most] Funds
- What Makes a Great Fund
- Starting Your Own Fund
- Investing Success in the New Era
- A Hybrid Approach

- What's Next?
- The Need for Constant Improvement & Innovation
- Balancing Disruption and Growth

- Fueling Innovation & Thinking Bigger
- World Changing Funds

- The Most In-Demand Skill
- 10 Ways to Boost Creative Thinking
- 7 Ways to Boost Strategic Thinking Capability
- Designing Your Thinking Space
- Scheduling Time to Think

Chapter 1:
The Journey

As far back as I can remember, I've always had a hustler's spirit, which has meant a lot of experimenting with different business ventures and investment models. That has yielded a lifetime of learning, a wealth of connections, and has led me to an incredible place.

I share the story of my real estate investing journey so that you can see what has driven the leaps I've made. And also to show you that if I can do it, then you are capable of even greater success. And if you learn these lessons early and you can skip to being an intelligent strategic investor instead of having to go through much of the trial and error I did.

I'm in a Great Space

In life, business, and my investments, I'm in a great place. I can say that I'm in the best place of my life so far, and it's not just about the money.

Not too long ago I restructured the company to take our investment fund ventures to a whole new level. It's so great when you and your team share great energy and synergy and are able to multiply what you each are capable of as a result.

My latest real estate fund takes a hybrid approach to investing across the real estate spectrum with real estate mortgage notes and tangible assets. We've rolled out new branding, brought in new team members, and have been making incredible connections as we travel around the country to various events. It's an amazing time.

More importantly, I'm training two young entrepreneurs and strategic investors. Those are my two boys, who are 10 and 16. We're enjoying family business meetings, experimenting with money management through allowances, building good habits, practicing visualization, and they're even taking on real estate jobs and getting out on work-sites.

Outside of those things, I occasionally teach on financial literacy in my home town at Essex County College in Newark as a way to give back. I'm still living with my mom. Okay okay, she actually moved in with us. And I think it's great! Now I have time to work on personal goals, keep a good routine with my daily rituals, and have the freedom to get out and enjoy life. The big difference today is, that I turned things around and have designed my life putting my family and personal objectives first. And then built my business and work around that. That's possible, first because it is necessary and I prioritize it, and secondly, thanks to the investments I've made and my business model.

Success Requires Strategy

To achieve great financial success and to sustain it, along with the lifestyle you love, it takes discipline and strategy.

Anyone can have a one hit wonder and make some fast cash. Keeping it is a whole different game. Real success demands thinking big, long, wide, and taking a lot into account - but it's worth it. You don't have to be a genius – in fact, our subconscious naturally prompts us. Often, we confuse this prompting with fear or a roadblock. Masked as doubt, most people either let it paralyze them or ignore it and charge ahead blindly.

Those that have struggled with really believing they can achieve massive success or with procrastination will love my book, The Tire Kicker. I've typically been one to push ahead and grab the bull by the horns. That's given me the advantage of trying many different things. I believe it has helped speed up my learning, even if it meant learning some tough lessons along the way.

What I've learned is that success isn't just about hard work, having a magical idea, or dumb luck. It is about being disciplined and strategic. It's about bringing together the best of multiple worlds.

Starting Out

I still remember mom feeding us ramen noodles for dinner. Growing up in 'Brick City,' NJ, there were days we didn't even have electricity. I can remember plenty of candle light dinners, and I'm not talking about the romantic type. Things were tough. With two brothers and two sisters, there were a lot of mouths to feed. I still remember the embarrassment of mom sending me to the store with food stamps. I'd walk and walk and wait around until I was sure my friends had checked out, or weren't in the store and the coast was clear. I didn't want them to know we were on food stamps. Still, to this day those memories drive me to ensure my children never have to deal with that. Despite raising us on her own, my mother still managed to send us to a private religious school, and was serious about education, values, and instilling a love of learning. That's a foundation that can make all the difference in a child and a generation.

On the weekends, we really got to flex and hone our entrepreneurial spirit. My younger brother and I would compete at what started out as my mom's side hustle, the flea market. We were just 10 and 8 at the time and at first were dragged along. And then it turned into a contest to see which one could sell more stuff. To the point that we wouldn't just wait for chance. In a moment that forced us to see what could be done, we'd get ahead of the crowd by going across the street to meet customers before they even got into the market. This was my first memory of our mom really giving us the idea of making our own money.

I landed my real first job at KFC at fourteen. By 19, my love for cars took me to a body shop, turning my passion into income. Through diligence and saving, I eventually became part owner. Later, I sold my share. At 20, I ran into a childhood friend who'd cashed in at a telecom company, so, I went to work as a telemarketer - a corporate job that provided benefits. I felt eager; I felt the hustle. Within a few months, the company promoted me to night manager.

I out-worked everyone, and earned a position on the West Coast as Director of Sales. I had never been to California before, so the decision seemed big. Yet, I took the plunge. I sat down with the president, negotiated a better pay package, and made the leap.
It was during this time I heard about real estate investing from my older brother who was a loan officer. But he had to wait 30 days to get paid, and I wasn't with that at all. And I enjoyed the California sunshine too much.

After spending two years in the Golden State, I really wanted to pay my mom back for all she did for us as kids. So, I invested my money in a joint venture with her so she could open up a restaurant back in New Jersey.

A few years later, the telecom company moved me back to New Jersey and put me to work in the customer service department. This gave me the opportunity to see what happens after the sale is made, and how processes are put in place to keep the customer. This also sharpened my sales skills.

During this time, websites were new to the market so I left the company and got into tech by selling websites to people who had previously been relying on the Yellowbook to promote themselves. My next job landed me in a company analyzing SEC files and researching companies that were hurting financially. I helped those struggling businesses fix their situations by outsourcing their needs and liquidating their real estate to increase profits. I was good at it, but the more accounts I landed meant more people that had to be laid off at these firms. I was making great money, but did not enjoy that part of it.

My cousin, who was in the business, introduced me to real estate investing. Houses and the construction process had always intrigued me - all it took was one deal and I was hooked!

Flipping Houses & The Best Thing That Happened To Me

I did my first real estate deal with my cousin and made $30,000 within just two months. I'd never had a paycheck like that before. Despite how hard I'd always worked, this was some of the easiest money I'd ever made. I was sold.

I had just landed one of the biggest accounts with Sony Loews. This new account put me over the $150k year mark at the age of 25. At this time my boss had the brilliant idea of increasing my base salary while lowering my commission, which meant I would never hit that $150k mark unless I landed 3 more big accounts. Little did he know that I had fallen in love with real estate investing, and I could make that entire year's salary with just two property deals, so I quit my job.

I got busy learning all I could. My cousin handled the construction, and I worked on other parts of the business. I handled the financing, and educated first time home buyers and taught people about the investment of buying a home.

The market was hot, and we were making great money. We also helped many people in our community by employing them and rehabilitating homes in our community. I was making money and adding value to my community. Then one morning at the office in 2001, I got hit hard.

Until then, the money we were making was compelling, but more than that, I had fallen in love with the renovations and revitalizing our neighborhood with the process of taking something broken down and building it back up again. It was our ground zero, and it provided a great feeling of significance too.

This was what real estate experts call a 'C Class' neighborhood. It was a proverbial 'lions' den'. Unfortunately, one thing you learn when you start making money in real estate is that not everyone is happy about your success and envy takes over.

We did payroll for the contractors every Friday, in cash. Someone we worked with leaked that information to some of those haters.

That March morning in 2001 when I went to open up the office I was shot five times.

If you've never been shot, there isn't anything that hurts quite like it. Perhaps impaling yourself on a bed of nine inch nails or childbirth. Only, the healing process is a lot longer. It took six months to recover.

Yet, I can honestly say that this was one of the best things that happened to me. It was during that time I really learned the importance of two things. The first is the importance of who you associate with. The second is the importance of passive income. Income that will keep coming in, even if you are stuck on life support or bedridden for a year. Around this time, I also got introduced to Robert Allen's book on multiple streams of income. When I recovered, I went back to flipping houses, and I flipped a *lot* of them. It just seemed easy and the money was plentiful. I hated dealing with tenants and did not understand property management so I was 'smart' and diversified into multiple businesses. Among them I had a 25 chair hair salon, a car wash, and owned a transportation business for special needs kids. I was *incredibly* busy. This gave me the opportunity to generate income from other businesses, but it was by no means passive income. I worked my face off to build these business while flipping houses. I had no rental income because I did not want to deal with tenants. Yet, across these companies I had at least 54 employees. Employees in these types of businesses can often be even more draining than renters.

Crash!
Then 2008 came along. The world cracked open, the bottom fell out. I crashed and burned. No one was buying houses. No one

was loaning or borrowing money. It was really, really ugly out there.

A marriage went bad, and cash flow ground to a halt. I was so down in the dumps that I didn't even want to get out of bed.

It took me a while, before I got to the point where I just got so determined to do something. I was consumed with negative energy from other people in my non real estate ventures. I made a commitment to myself to find a way, and to succeed once again. I determined to make sure I surrounded myself with the right people, and to push away the toxic energy. I began to meditate and journal, and created other good habits such jogging in the morning.

While many people were still blaming the market and the banks, I decided to take ownership and responsibility for what was happening in my life. And so I became determined to learn more, and to look further ahead this time, while building sustainability into my business and investments and maintaining flexibility, but without being a slave to the money this time.

Before Discovering Debt

Before the crash I was always on the go. I was a car with no steering wheel though, being bumped into new directions by every pothole. I was extremely busy. Yet, despite doing well in many ways, I wasn't really taking control over my life, direction and finances. I was just on the rollercoaster for the ride, and I let others take the controls.

The crash created a wakeup call. It demanded investing time to get my mind right and a lot of self-searching. It meant reading

and meditating. Time to strategize how to never have my financial future or schedule in the hands of others or the market.
In the wake of the crash I was still running all of these other businesses. I evaluated each of them. I ranked them by how much of a time suck they were and the toxic energy they put in my life. I vowed to begin selling them off. One at a time I exited all of those extra companies.

I was still staying tuned into the real estate market. I even went to school and got my real estate license. I was looking to build more direct connections to REO realtors and banks. As many other investors have probably experienced though, being a realtor isn't all it's cracked up to be, and isn't nearly as great as just doing deals.

I ran into Nancy, another real estate investor, in the hall of records one day. She told me about an attorney who was hosting local seminars. I wasn't interested in being sold on anything. I pushed back, but she talked me into checking one out.
I took a leap of faith on her recommendation. I was surprised at how good it was. I found that contrary to the news media, the real estate market was still very much alive. The room was buzzing and vibrant and was home to a whole community and ecosystem. There were investors, vendors and hard money lenders there doing deals. The speaker was very informative, provided good educational content and provided some solid resources.

The attorney leading the event was mostly doing short sales at that time. At the end of the session he left those of us in attendance with, "You can pay me $6,000 and I'll mentor you on how to do short sales for yourself. Or, you can come work in my office on an internship program for 6 months, do the business and learn for free."

That reminded me of what I had read by Robert Kiyosaki (Rich Dad, Poor Dad). How he wanted to open a bakery. So, he went and took a job in a bakery working for someone else. He learned the business, the systems and the vendors. Then he took all that knowledge and opened his own bakery.

So, despite all I had accomplished before I pushed myself to be humble and decided to give the strategy a shot. This attorney was doing around six closings a week, which is a pretty good pace for a small business if you knew what it takes to pull everything together. So, I went in with an open mind, I watched, I learned, I listened, I stayed coachable. Being in that active environment, where things were happening, deals were closing and money was moving revived my excitement for the business. That proved pivotal for my next leap.

After 6 months I opened my own office. It began as a paralegal support office. Since I had seen the challenges of trying to manage short sales first hand, I knew how to process files and develop systems. If the attorneys, who were jumping into the short sale and loan modification business by the hundreds, would outsource the back office work to my company and team, they could work far more efficiently and profitably.

I got more involved with negotiating directly with the banks on these files. And that opened up a new world for me. It opened my mind to the internal working of the banks, including trying to arrange bridge loans for pools of notes.

Discovering Debt

Banks were in a mess. They weren't helping people. Even when they needed and wanted to cut deals to grant short sales and loan modifications, they were very disorganized and almost impossible to work with, which cost a lot of people their homes. Far more than the media was really publicizing or the data was showing. The banks needed help, and homeowners needed help.

I drove my kids to school in the morning. In between challenging them with mental math games, I'd take jkbusiness calls. And my sons would overhear me trying to help people while negotiating with the lenders. They could see the pressure on me and the struggle. One exasperating morning in the car I announced "these banks don't want to help people." Then one of my sons simply replied "Why don't you just become the bank?"

"Impossible!" I said.

With an unforgettable look of sheer shock on his face, my son said "What?!"

Here was the father that spent every day for years trying to pump these children up. Pushing their entrepreneurial spirit, I preached how they can achieve anything they put their mind to, and be whatever they want to be. I drummed it into them so much that they believed it. For a moment, I burst that bubble.

Never again will I say the 'I____" word.

If you ever hear it slip out of my lips, please feel free to give me a quick kick to the shins or splash of hot sauce in the eye.

It was a true light bulb moment for me. I had been saying one thing, but I wasn't really living it to the edge, or thinking big enough.

So, I decided to find out how banks were created and formed. My preconception was that because of their size, it would be extremely difficult to start a bank. Or at least be the one with the power to personally help homeowners when they ran into genuine hardships with their mortgages.

Still, I began researching banks and their structures. Along with many different sized banks, as well as private banks, I discovered private placements as a vehicle to raise capital. I worked with an investor that had fund experience - acting as the bank to fund short sale and mortgage loans purchases, in addition to other paper. I went all in with a lot of research and learning, talking to SEC attorneys, and learning how to set things up.

It was then I discovered debt investing, and reinvented how to use it. Until then it was virtually unheard of for regular investors to be able to buy loan notes from banks. In 2011 and 2012, this was true even at REIA meetings. Yet, there was this huge need and opportunity to profit, while really providing a valuable and much needed service.

So, I started investing in real estate mortgage notes - buying defaulted mortgage loans from banks and other lenders at deep discounts. They began selling them at pennies on the dollar, and in bulk. Many homeowners had found themselves in high cost loans that they just couldn't afford anymore due to the economic turmoil. Some had been trying to fix things with their lenders, but just couldn't navigate the awful systems that were in place.

Others just couldn't catch up and needed an exit. The ones that could catch up were desperate to save their homes, and were only glad to have someone that could really help. It was a win-win-win.

I developed the same love and passion for the note business as for flipping houses and other types of real estate. My why was still the same too. Yes, there is great money in it - but there are plenty of ways to just make money. I had a burning desire to help others and do something significant. The days of growing up in 'Brick City' in the 80s were still vivid in my mind. One of my big goals has always been to go back and revitalize those run-down neighborhoods. Through rehabbing, flipping, rentals and notes, I have been able to help good people stay in their homes, give families a second chance, employ people who just want to work to provide for their families, and to bring buildings to life. And all while providing safe housing and bringing positive life to those streets. That is hands down far more rewarding than any sum of money. Plus, if you can get paid for doing what you love too, it's not really 'work', it's living your passion.

Becoming the Bank

In many ways, I found note investing even better than fixing and flipping houses or being a landlord. For the most part, you never have to worry about maintenance, all the expenses, the risks and hassles of rehabbing, or whether the market is up or down. You hold the paper and just get paid passive income month after month. When borrowers run into trouble, there are many ways to work with them. We've modified loans, cut interest rates and payments, waived back fees, and even dropped the amounts owed. Often, we've even counseled them on how to get their finances in order, save money on living expenses, and have even helped many get jobs. Even when you exhaust those options, you are typically buying these loans at such a discount that you can turn around and sell them for a fast profit, or can work with the homeowner to take over the property and get them out of debt. Then you can either put in a tenant or spruce the house up and flip it. There are so many exit strategies.

People, who needed to find a way back after having their finances ripped apart and wanted a way to make more money, noticed.. So I created National Note Group as investment company that would facilitate the purchase of loans in even larger bulk quantities at even better discounts. It also enabled individual investors and other groups to participate in the success and profits, by giving them access to our notes and systems. It educated thousands of other investors through online information, coaching calls, and lunch and learn sessions. I found that I was being called on to speak on note investing across the country. It wasn't long before it only made sense to put this all in a book. Turning Distress into Success hit Amazon and has been there to enlighten others about these investment options, teach them how to do it for themselves, and even how to raise capital and launch their own funds.

The company quickly grew and grew, requiring more staff, new technology, and more systems to handle all the business that was coming in, in addition to the millions of dollars being raised, invested, and paid out. We had become the 'bank'. We were investing in loans, giving individuals a way to make great returns on their money passively, and we were really helping borrowers.

Unleashing the Hybrid Strategy

In the last quarter of 2015, I attended a major industry conference with many big institutional players in attendance - including public REITs and other large fund managers. They had invited me to moderate a panel on notes. It was a real honor to be credited with adding value to that group.

I walked into that event with a personal goal of doing 10 house flips that year. That's outside of the business and funds I was running. Prior to 2008 I had been doing closer to 30 houses a year. To be honest, the note business made me soft! It was just too easy. I was essentially able to wield millions of dollars in mortgage notes from just my laptop and mobile phone.

At that event there were guys buying, renovating and holding 10,0000 single family properties each. It was a great kick in the backside that not only inspired me, but put a battery in my back. It spurred me to set bigger goals. In a recent blog post I detailed how that led me to completing 30 rehabs in the following 30 months after walking out of that event.

It turned me on to taking advantage of more of the REO opportunities on the table. I had the connections to acquire great property deals, but had just been so focused on the notes. And it gave me another light bulb moment - the idea to try and create a vehicle for both notes and hard real estate. I spent the next year on due diligence, tax planning and structures. During that time I began allowing private investors who weren't a perfect fit for the existing note fund to participate in my private deals. Individuals poured in within anywhere from $25k from their IRA to $150k to invest, and within months that grew to $5M.

I had begun working with an SEC attorney to develop a new platform and private placement materials to bring this all together.

In early 2017, we began rolling out this new fund. It has been very well received and continues the great success and performance we achieved with previous note funds. There are significant differences though.

Whereas previous real estate funds and investments were focused on real estate notes, and especially on non-performing secured mortgage notes, the new real estate fund is a hybrid. Inside this fund portfolio is mixed:

- Secured real estate notes, performing and non-performing
- Hard real estate, assets from flips and rentals
- Tax liens

This provides the benefits of value positions and cash flow from existing real estate notes, in addition to the advantages of renovating and repositioning physical real estate and holding income producing properties, all in one fund.

There are two main reasons for this big change. The first is that, while I have been one of the most vocal advocates for note investing for years (and still am), I have also been investing in flips and income properties for myself, outside of my business. So I thought to myself, "why am I still profiting from these other strategies personally, and not giving other investors the benefit of participating in the profits, opportunities, and our team's expertise?" The possibility was there, now that I had the framework in place to do it efficiently, consistently, and at scale.

16

The second reason is for diversification. Throughout my journey so far, I have time and again discovered that having multiple streams of income is vital. Yet, I also found that I kept being drawn back to real estate, and have been endowed with a great gift for it. I came to the conclusion that it's best to diversify, so that your portfolio is always firing at its maximum capacity, without unnecessary risk. And at the same time, it's far more efficient and profitable to master one field, versus trying to learn and manage varied businesses in different industries. I became a strategic and hybrid investor.

Whether you are an investor in the fund or not, I firmly believe that everyone needs to become a more strategic, hybrid investor. Whatever your preferences, the following pages will empower you to get clarity on what you really want, how to craft your own custom plan, enhance your strategic thinking, overcome challenges, understand investments, innovate, and even become aware of how your investments can help you impact your community and the world for the better.

Chapter 2:
What Do You Want?

You've got to Know Where You are Going

In order to get where you want to go, you have to have real clarity about what it is that you want.

If you follow two different lines on a compass which are relatively close, you'll see how dramatically different your results can be. A few degrees off on a different tangent can send you off to another country or a completely different continent!

You can bet that this becomes far more disparate when you don't have much of a vision at all. Invest the time you need to get clarity on this. What is your ultimate goal? What does life look like when you arrive there? What specific metrics are you shooting for? What are some key milestones you desire to achieve, and when should you accomplish them by? All of this will play into what types of investments you make and how you choose them.

The Change You Wish to Make

Deep down, there is something we all wish we could change. This could simply be a desired change in lifestyle, finances, and/ or relationships. Many are passionate about broader and larger changes. That may translate into helping to turn around their neighborhood or city, improving the environment, helping the homeless and those in need of good, healthy and affordable housing, or creating a financial surplus to help squash the world's poverty and water crises.

Some leave these aspirations to later in life. They put them to the back of their minds, with the idea that they'll start tackling or contributing to the cause once they've 'made it'. Tony Robbins, for example, feeds millions of people in the cities he visits. Then there is John D. Rockefeller who began giving a part of his earnings from his very first paycheck.

When I got into this business, I was excited to go back to and revitalize the neighborhood I was from, restoring the community. Being out there making neighboring homes useful again and providing needed relief to homeowners felt like I was putting my Superman cape on every day.

If you follow the blog, you'll also find a piece on how I work with and manage contractors. This can be a very challenging part of the business. At the same time, it's an equally great opportunity to make a difference. Contractors aren't used to being treated well. I too expect a lot from them. Yet, I like them to win also. I like to see them succeed, and not just put food on the table and keep the lights on, but to do more and be able to really show up when it counts for their family and to give their kids opportunities to excel. So, you don't have to quit working, sell everything and go volunteer for the rest of your life after all! We definitely need volunteers. There are however, so many ways you can make a difference just with how you interact with others and invest your money on a daily basis alone.

The problem with pushing off your bigger wishes to contribute and have a positive impact is that sometimes you never make it to that day. Others wake up one day, shocked to find that they have spent the last few decades fueling the problem they've most wanted to change. It could be waking up to realizing your prized over-sized SUV has been poisoning the air for your kids for the last 10 years. It could be the realization that the bank you've been supporting with your deposits and borrowing from has been defrauding millions of lesser fortunate customers. Or the company whose stock you invested in has been involved in child labor overseas, or putting faulty materials into homes and apartment buildings. Things are finally changing in this respect though. Individual investors are finally awakening to the fact that what they invest in has big and broad impacts. Whatever you care about, and whatever your values are, make sure you invest in line with that. Choose companies, assets, and managers who share your vision.

The #1 Rule

While this really comes second to investing in line with your values, leading investors like Warren Buffett say the number one rule of investing is not to lose money.

The wealthy are sometimes criticized and ridiculed for making poor investments with very low yields. Part of this is that they are busy and defer their decisions to others, or aren't actively investing their own money. The other half is that they understand the importance of preserving their capital. It's not worth taking on extreme risk for the promise of 70% growth, if it could mean losing all of your capital. If you lose your capital, you have nothing to invest. It's better to get 10% returns, and be confident in the security of your investment capital. Even if you break even, at least you live to invest another day. You may diversify, and have riskier, higher growth potential investments balance out more stable ones in your portfolio, but you don't want to invest so wildly that you are just gambling. This is one of the reasons I love real estate, as do most billionaires. It can offer good growth and yield potential, but also offers concrete security. Stocks can be vaporized, a startup can fail to gain traction, gold bars can be stolen, but land will always be there. Be assured, whatever they invest in, the savviest investors look for opportunities where they have out-sized security cushions.

The 100 Year Plan

Strategic investing is critical for achieving your objectives. At its best, it brings together your values, your biggest goals and aspirations and keeps what you already have safe. However, according to Bill Gates, all too often we overestimate what we can achieve in one year, and underestimate what we can achieve in ten. We've also sadly been trained to be very short sighted. Most people have five year plans, and they are super proud of them. Yet, the most successful investors and organizations continue to be those with 100 year plans. My friend Tim says that the big problem with the cliché five-year plan is, What do you do when you hit the five-year mark? Either you take too much risk to hit all your goals within the five years, and may find yourself in financial trouble before you hit the mark. Or you have an unsustainable financial situation once you hit month 60.

While none of us may live another 100 years, our businesses and kids might. A legacy is probably one of your top goals, right? By planning long, we also build in more sustainability in order to make steady gains that we actually get to keep and pass on. You'll certainly have goals you want to achieve much sooner, but looking at the bigger picture enables us to invest strategically to get and keep what we want in the long term too.

Balance on the Journey

We've been talking about some pretty big and long goals. Though we also need to be able to enjoy the journey. If we do, then it is more likely we will stick to the course, and get where we want to be, financially and with our desires. Plus, the journey is the best part!

No one wants to be on their deathbed, before they hit those final miles, and be full of regret that they didn't enjoy themselves, spend time with those they love, cross off those bucket list items, or create valuable memories others will carry on. This is all a part of truly being a well-rounded strategic investor. So, how do you find balance?

Time blocking down time and vacation time is a must. Don't compromise. Then make room in your daily and weekly schedule to get out and get balanced when you need it. Whatever type of work you do, you need breaks to refresh your mind, recharge, remember why you are doing what you are doing, and to live. I personally love spending time with my sons, as well as trying out all types of adrenaline pumping activities. Find what works for you. You might even make a short list of activities you want to try; i.e. golf, yoga, poker, catching a show, a country you want to visit, or trying a new restaurant. Put them in a bowl or on the fridge and pick one to do each week or month.

Do not underestimate the importance of this balance. It can be the best part of life, and avoiding burnout is critical for sticking to your big vision.

The Power of Sharing Your Goals

Once you know what you want, and you've set the goals that give you a tangible vision, share it. From experience, I can tell you there is great power in sharing with others.

Some people operate from a mindset of fear and scarcity. They spend so much time trying to protect what they have, when in reality they have no control, or in guarding 'secrets' which really aren't secrets at all, or in being paranoid that others will copy or compete with them. The truth, as I've found, is that the most successful and happy people are those who enjoy sharing. They aren't afraid to share their success tips and visions. Often that's actually what brings those things about.

Three things happen when you share.

1. You Put it into Action

When you speak it, you put it out there into the universe, and begin making it a reality. You can call this the law of attraction, or positive thinking, or faith. You don't even have to understand how or why it works. Just try it, and you'll see.

2. You Begin Gaining Traction

When you put your ideas out there, things start to happen. You personally start taking more action, and can make more progress than you think, just by sharing your ideas. You might be surprised at who shares your ideals and will want to help or can connect you with others who can help. You only get these benefits when you share. So share consistently.

3. You Create Accountability Partners

Sharing your goals creates accountability partners. This might begin with friends, family, co-workers, local acquaintances, or industry professionals. You don't even need to be actively trying to recruit these people as partners, clients, or board members. Once you've mentioned it, they'll often ask you how it is going when you run into them. If you know your Uber driver is going to ask about your progress every morning, your coworker is going to quiz you at happy hour on Friday, your mom is going to want the latest update at the next holiday dinner, and a local professional is going to call and email you every quarter to see how it's going, you are going to be far more motivated and in the mode to clock progress than if no one is asking. This also gives you a warm opportunity to solicit help and referrals from these people as needs arise.

Our company is the perfect example of this in action. Several years ago, I went to lunch with a friend and laid out my vision over sushi. I remember saying to her, "This is what I'm going to do…" While the exact tactics hadn't been nailed down at the time, I shared that my goals were to raise $2M, and then eventually flip an entire fund. I put in six figures of my own money, and my friend became the first investor. Then she became one of our core team members. Everything happened exactly as I had said. We hit that $2M milestone in the first year. Then we, as a company, began sharing our progress, successes, inside information, and opportunities with as many other investors and individuals as we could. And fund after fund has been a success. Now we are dealing in the tens of millions of dollars, and have launched the new hybrid fund, which is going to be even bigger.

Chapter 3:
The Game Plan

Laying Out the Game Plan

Now that you've gotten this far in the book you probably already have some ideas sparking. You've got a vision forming, some goals and a working list of fun and exciting things you are going to do on the journey. You're thinking long and are itching to really dig in! This is when you want to start formulating a real plan, or at least dust off and upgrade the ones you may have had before.

You've got direction, but now it needs to be focused and broken down into specific goals and actions that will help the end vision become a reality. It's like being a football coach. The coach knows he wants to win the season. That vague goal alone isn't enough though, right? He should visualize winning the Super Bowl, and be positive about that outcome. Yet to get there, he has to win some games. He needs a diverse team of carefully chosen players who have the capacity to take the team there too. He'll probably need some junior coaches as well, in addition to investing in the right players, and nurturing them along the way. He may even need to make some trades. Add to all that the strategizing involved in the actual games. Not to mention that different games will have different tactics on top of that.

The point is that we all need a game plan. Without it, we're just betting it all on hope. And that's not a winning strategy.

What it Looks Like

Physically laying out your game plan makes all the difference. It can be digitally on your laptop, in the cloud, or on your phone. Or it can be on good old-fashioned paper. Find what works for you. There are three main categories to account for here:

1. Your ultimate goals
2. The strategies you'll use to get there
3. The action steps you need to focus on to move forward

Some people need intense organization and detail. Others simply need a direction and targets to shoot for, at least in the beginning as they work out the details. Generally, the more specific you are in your plan, the better. Yet, it is equally important not to let this slow you down and cause you to miss crucial opportunities and time.

Some people are great at quickly and accurately forecasting figures. They like to have the rest of their lives planned out to the dollar. They know when they'll be going on vacation for the next five years, where to, and already have a 'jar' accumulating the funds needed for it. Others don't even have next month mapped out.

The point here is that not everything always goes according to plan perfectly. Markets change, new technology comes along, income may fluctuate, unexpected expenses can come up, and so on. So, you may have a more specific immediate plan, and more generic markers over future years. When I got started in real estate I was working with two year plans. That's as far as I could accurately forecast ahead, or thought I needed to. That has since evolved into five year plans, and ten year plans, with an eye on the much larger picture. I set out verticals for business goals, savings, and personal goals. I focus on realistic goals, which allow me to gain and keep up the momentum.

Some ways to lay this out may include:

- Using Excel spreadsheets
- Financial budgeting forms
- Retirement investment planning forms
- Bulleted to-do lists
- Business plan style documents and executive summaries
- Simplified one sheet, single view plans

Many who are reading this may find it incredibly eye opening to complete a financial budget. If you've never done so, you may have a big awakening moment as to where your money is going, why you are constantly coming up short, and where you might want to make adjustments.

Simplicity is important too. Airbnb was featured in Fast Company for creating its global domination plan across multiple channels, on just one sheet of paper. If it gets too complicated to fit, then maybe it's just too complicated.

What is critical is that your game plan includes how much you need financially when you hit the end zone, some clear milestones to clock your progress by, general strategies for getting there, and the next tactic you will explore and engage in to get some forward momentum.

Choose a format. Start working with it. Tweak as you go.

Getting a Second Opinion
It's always wise to get a second opinion. It doesn't matter how

high our IQs are, how much research we've done, or how obvious or genius our plans appear, it is always wise to get a second opinion.

This applies to personal financial plans, investment moves, and business plans. We are often too close and can suffer from tunnel vision. It doesn't matter how many millions I make, how many years I've done it, and how well things have worked, I'll always look for second opinions.

We compare clothes shops, mobile phone and car deals. We usually get second opinions on even minor medical choices like supplements, dental work, and OTC medicines. Why on earth wouldn't we do the same for our finances, when our entire futures and legacies are at stake?

We can solicit feedback from people like:

- Parents
- Kids
- Spouses
- Partners
- Friends
- Coworkers
- Financial planners
- Attorneys
- Accountants
- Board members
- Team members

Obviously, it's important to balance the feedback we get according to who it's from. We need to weigh that input based on source biases. For example, you may know your attorney is overly detailed and likes to clock extra hours. Or your brother in law may always be ultra conservative financially, whereas your sister may be the opposite. One financial advisor may have their own agenda in wanting to sell you a different product, and so on. While another contact may spot a small tweak you can use to make it even better. Just calculate these factors in. At a minimum, this is a part of sharing your goals and putting them out there as we discussed earlier. It may help you hone your ideas, or even get you some extra backing you weren't expecting. You might send more details about a specific item to some of these people, ie. the information on an investment to your IRA custodian to approve versus just calling your mom and saying, "Hey mom, I'm thinking about investing in mortgage notes because of 'xyz', what do you think?" Ultimately though, make your own decision.

Putting it into Play

Now that you have a game plan, you need to start putting it into play.

There are three main factors here:
1.   Keeping up your momentum
2.   Having clear, actionable steps to focus on
3.   Keeping the time to make progress

You have to stay driven if you want to keep making progress toward your goals. Just having a number in the back of your mind, or a business plan in an envelope collecting dust in a drawer isn't enough to keep most people going. It's too easy to lose sight of the goal, lose passion for it, and more commonly – to get distracted.

We can't afford to get off track and take detours as we only have so many days. I'm blessed to be doing what I love every day, and it is all a part of my financial and strategic investment plan. I'm living in my zone. I thrive on doing new deals every day, and feel great that I am getting up in the morning to help others do the same.

You may not yet be living out your dream all day, every day, but you can start to. You can start to experience that passion for life, fulfillment, and happiness a little more each day as you stay focused, and make progress. One of the most effective ways to achieve this is through creating daily success habits. I spend time every morning meditating. I take time to practice the visualization of my goals. It sets me up right for the day. It fills me with passion and keeps me focused on what's important, increasing the manifestation of my goals. Using goal or vision boards is still one of the most powerful and effective ways to do this. Some people add yoga, journaling, taking a 'power hour' with music to psych themselves up, and practicing gratitude.

Today, many of us are mobile and that's great. It can make getting into a good rhythm challenging though, especially at first. Get into a routine of good habits by replacing traditional tools with an online journal, alerts on your phone, and using your laptop screensaver and background as your vision board. Use your smartwatch to keep you focused on your goals, or keep a card in your wallet with your goals on it. Read it every morning, when you are in traffic, when waiting for the train or a meeting, and before you go to sleep. This will all keep your motivation and energy up, which are necessary to move forward.

We also need to take practical steps because at the end of the day, it all comes down to action. Aside from losing focus, the most common reason people don't gain traction toward their goals or stay consistent is that they keep getting stuck on what's next. They know where they are, and where they want to go, but lack the clear steps to bridge that gap. Champion this, and keep up the pace by breaking those goals into easy action steps.

Break the big goals into major milestones. Then break those milestones into smaller accomplishments that you can check off, and then down to easy actions you can cross off on a daily or weekly basis.

Here is a rough example:

> Big goal: Have $100,000 in annual passive income ($8,333 per month)
> Milestones: Create $12k in annual passive income
> To-do: Make an investment which produces $1,000 in monthly income (then replicate)
> Next action step: Research passive income investments – read the Hybrid book

Break it down to the one next step you can take. Schedule time to work on this next step each day. It can be in the evening, on your lunch break, or first thing in the morning.

Chapter 4:
Investing

Why is it so important to invest anyway? What priority should investing take in our lives? Where do we begin with investing and diversifying investments?

This may all seem obvious to some, but remembering certain key factors can be critical in making intelligent money decisions.

The Need to Invest

The primary reason to invest is not even about making money. It is about protecting it. It is about protecting our freedom, wealth, and health. Simply saving alone isn't enough. In fact, it could be argued that once you exceed the equivalent of 3 to 6 months' worth of living expenses in savings that saving more can be counterproductive.

It is good to have an accessible cash reserve for urgent emergencies like running to the doctor, or fixing a flat tire, or covering the rent in case your paycheck gets held up. However, idle money is constantly going down in value. Time Money says even a low 2% to 3% rate of annual inflation will reduce the value of $1 to just 60 cents in 20 years. Often cash will devalue far faster than that[1]. If your investment returns or savings interest is not beating inflation when you include fees, then you are actually losing money. Imagine putting $10,000 in $100 bills under your bed. Then a few years from now pulling them out and finding

---

[1] http://time.com/money/collection-post/2791990/why-should-i-invest/

they are now all just $50 bills, and you only have $5,000. You'd be pretty mad and disappointed, right? That is the case with most bonds, CDs, and savings accounts today. Then there is the simple security issue. Cash under the mattress or even in a home safe is at high risk every day. There are risks of theft, fire, animals, and other disasters. Banks haven't proven to be solid either. Some have been so consistently unethical that placing deposits with them is crazy. There is also an added risk when savings exceed FDIC protection thresholds.

Multiplying what we have is the most common reason people invest. Whether you've got $5,000 or $250,000 above your basic cash cushion, you want to not only protect it, but multiply it. By investing in appreciating assets, or assets we can enhance the value of over time, we build wealth. This may be done directly and privately with whatever you have, or using debt or equity leverage to speed up results and minimize risk.

Tax reduction is another smart reason to invest. By using vehicles such as 401ks, IRAs, Roths, Healthcare Savings Accounts (HSAs), and Education Savings Accounts (ESAs), we can not only multiply our money, but we get to keep more of it, as we gain deductions or breaks on income taxes. We'd all like to keep more of every paycheck we get, right? Even better, you get to use that money to make more money.

Typically, investors pay less in taxes on investment income than other types of income too. Using some of these tax saving vehicles, individual investors may pay 28% to over 40% less in taxes than others. Add that up! Then add up all the extra money you can make with that money. What if you had 40% more money to invest each year? Would that make a difference in your finances and future?

Investing also means maximizing the ROI on our time and energy. The returns you get mean you ultimately get a lot more for every hour you put in. You can turn the hours you've clocked on a job into far more than your hourly rate.   One investment move that yields just a thousand dollars per year, and took you less than an hour to do, is far more than most people can ever make, including highly paid doctors and lawyers.

Most important of all, investing can deliver passive income. It doesn't matter what job you have, eventually you'll cap out on what people will pay you per hour. With this earned income you are also limited to how many hours you can work and for how long. Just putting in some overtime, working nights, weekends and holidays isn't going to dramatically get you ahead financially. Investing for passive income and returns completely changes these dynamics though. All of a sudden you have income being generated and coming in on your days off and when you sleep. It is paid sick, personal, and vacation days. It means money coming in even when you can't get to work, find a job, and when you retire. We never know when those days are coming. If we wait till they are upon us it can be too late for investing. If you've just been laid off, are stuck in a hospital, or are forced into early retirement, there are going to be a lot of other more immediate demands on any cash and capital you have.

Invest First

Be an investor first, not a consumer. They say millionaires live like they are broke, and broke people spend like they are millionaires. This may be a slight exaggeration, but there is a distinct difference in mindset. One which helps the rich get richer, and means the poor keep getting poorer. Most notably it is about choosing to invest first and spend what is left, versus shopping first and investing if there is ever anything left, which there normally isn't.

Now, don't get this confused. I don't mean that you have to live like a monk in a barren cave and walk everywhere with bare feet, while only eating plain rice. There are many great benefits in minimalism. Yet, life should be enjoyable and fun too, and it is great to spoil those we love. In many cases there are things we can spend on that are material, but can be investments too. However, there is a critical and urgent need to get financial priorities right.

There are two big differences in how the wealthy think about spending:

1. They don't spend to make people think more of them
2. They invest first, and allow their investments to pay for their luxuries

This isn't just about those who already have billions in the bank either. This is also about those who are on the right track. They are those who don't feel they have to spend $150k on a car just to boost their own egos, or lease themselves up to the neck to feel better about themselves. For someone with such a mindset, there will never be enough money or toys to make them feel good for long.

The truly wealthy and financially free spend within their means. They invest first, from the top of their income. Then they let the returns and passive income coming in pay for those other things. Invest your money too, and have it working for you, rather than blowing it just to show off. Though I am certainly all about enjoying the rewards you create and celebrating successes, I just believe in getting that spending in the right order and in perspective.

I'm not going to pretend that this is easy to do nowadays. There is constant and deafening pressure to do the opposite and obtain instant gratification at the expense of the rest of your life. There is also a lot of deceptive marketing and peer pressure which never stop. It takes a lot of willpower to resist unnecessarily trading up that perfectly fine 11 month old vehicle or phone or home to the next model. Just remember the big picture though, and keep in mind who it really benefits. Will the next dollar you spend really benefit you and your family in the long run, or is it actually just fattening the investment returns and retirement savings of someone else who probably really doesn't need it? Make no mistake about it - there is a battle going on over your financial future. Make sure you are winning it. Even if that means you need to tune out and listen to some different voices or gain more quiet time to focus on what is really important.

Invest first. Put it into solid assets which can appreciate in value and throw off good yields. Then have fun with the returns.

Portfolio Mix

We need to invest. We need to have some diversification in our investments to be strategic and build in sustainability. So, what types of things might we invest in? How much of our investment dollars should go where?

There are numerous potential things to invest in, including:

- Stocks
- Debt
- Bonds
- Real estate
- Precious metals
- Private equity (i.e. startups)
- Certificates of Deposit (CDs) and cash

There is a lot of debate about the place these different types of investments have in an individual's investment portfolio, and how capital should be distributed among them.

As I was writing this book, I went to a lunch meeting with an investor interested in participating in our trademarked, diversified hybrid model fund. In such meetings, I like to find out where investors are with their portfolio to see if it's a good fit. To my surprise he told me he was already making 16% to 18% on some of his investments. So, I asked why he was so interested in investing with us for an 11% base return. At 75 years of age, he said he recognized the wisdom and need for strategic investment. He was already spreading his money across different funds that do similar things to ours, but all individually. In other words, real estate and hard money lending funds. The reason he came to us is because he saw we offered all of this together in one hybrid fund.

There may be different answers for those seeking to diversify. Some of the factors to consider when allocating your investments into different buckets include the following:
- Age
- Risk tolerance

- Need for growth
- How much you have to invest
- Time to retirement
- Performance projections for different asset classes
- Goals: income, preservation, and growth

The two main types of advice individuals will find online and at traditional stock brokers are:
- Allocation by age
- Allocation by risk tolerance

Most calculators and options are only broken down by 3 choices:
1. Stocks (equities)
2. Fixed income (i.e. bonds)
3. Cash

These suggestions range from heavily weighting a portfolio with stocks if investors are willing to be very aggressive and take on a lot of risk, to being extremely conservative and severely limiting positive return potential with bonds.

For example:

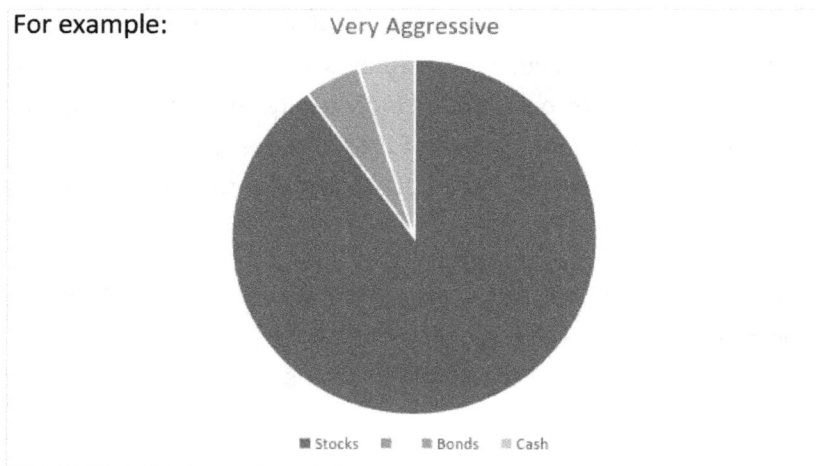

Very Aggressive

Stocks   Bonds   Cash

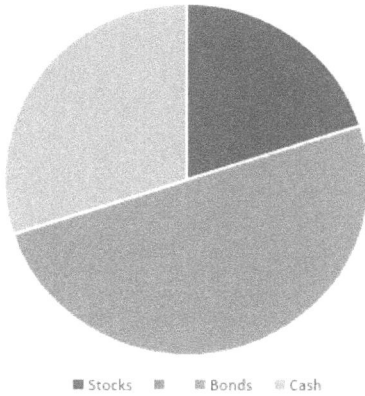
Very Conservative

Stocks ■ ■ Bonds Cash

Unfortunately, this space is dominated by a few firms with very biased and self-serving views. These examples really don't take into account the full range or investments out there, and do not provide anywhere near the depth or breadth of diversification individuals need to be safe and profitable.

A better and more diverse example may be:

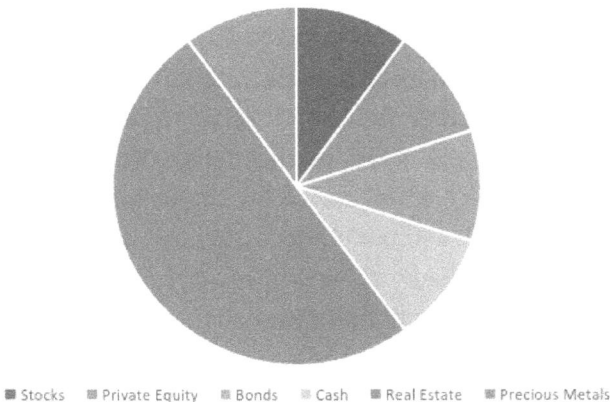
Better Diversified

■ Stocks ■ Private Equity ■ Bonds Cash ■ Real Estate ■ Precious Metals

Real Estate Diversification

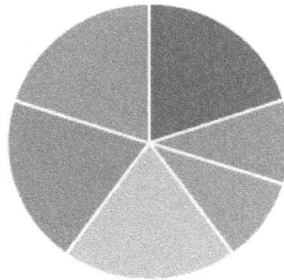

- Residential income property
- Multifamily Property
- Commercial Property
- Fix & Flips
- 1st Mtg. Notes
- 2nd Mtg. Notes

You can go even deeper by investing in different types of notes, in different price ranges, in different geographic locations, with a diverse mix of tenants. This delivers deep and broad diversification, along with the benefits of mastery in one major field (real estate). Note that whatever factors can drive gains in other asset classes also affect these real estate sectors, providing similar benefits, but while staying in your strong zone.

For example, if I am holding multifamily apartments in my portfolio which serve the tech crowd, their values go up when tech goes up. When retail does well, so does mixed-use and retail space. When stocks are up, luxury properties are more in demand. When the stock market fails, affordable rentals and discounted notes are hot, and so on. I can benefit from every turn in the economy, without unnecessary exposure to loss in the stock market, all while staying in my circle of mastery. You can also streamline the entire process and minimize costs by having a mix of these investments in one real estate fund.

Pros & Cons of Major Asset Classes

Each asset class and type of investment has its own pros and cons.

Stocks

Stocks are a common default investment when people are too lazy to put any time into thinking about what they are investing in. Stocks can yield good returns if you can time them just right. Real estate has typically beat stocks though. However, if you have no time, want to let someone else manage your money, and are willing to gamble for the potential upside and accept the risks, it can be an easy option. The major drawbacks are the extreme volatility and the zero downside protection. If a company goes bust, these days you don't even have a paper stock certificate as a token of your investment. Often there is little correlation between real fundamentals and share prices, which can make it even tougher to predict.

Precious Metals

Metals like gold and silver are seen as a safe zone. If the currency becomes worth less than the paper it is printed on, stocks tank, and people fearing a zombie apocalypse grab gold. It is a tangible asset you can hold and carry around, and will probably always have some type of value. The downside is that there is normally little room for growth, no income, and it can be very difficult to find a trusted source to acquire quality metals from.

Tech Startups

Private equity investments in early stage startups are still popular. Some of the buzz about this type of investment has died down, yet many dream of being an early investor in the next Facebook. The upside can be 100x, if you hit a winner. The downside is that these can be very illiquid investments which tie up capital for years, with no real resale market. Even the best venture capitalists will tell you that very, very few of these investments pay off. That one win has to be able to cover the losses on your other bets.

CDs & Cash

As discussed earlier, CDs, cash savings and bonds can deliver very low returns. Often, they will be net negative once you calculate taxes, fees, and inflation. There may be a place for some of these investments though, as everyone should certainly have access to enough cash to get them through a few months of unexpected expenses or absence of income.

Real Estate

It's no secret that I love investing in real estate. To be completely transparent, it is true that real estate asset values can fluctuate, just as with any other investment. A property may need to be sold or leased to realize yields and cash profits. There are many ways to invest in and profit from real estate though. The most common benefits that attract investors include: a range of organic and advanced tax advantages, high return potential, having a tangible asset as security, passive income, and the ability to simultaneously generate cash flow and wealth.

Chapter 5:
Eternal Optimism & Rising Above the Challenges

We may put all of the things covered in this book so far into play, and still have opportunity to deal with some challenges. That's okay. Tests will come. Having the right mindset, being prepared, knowing your plan, and having the right infrastructure can make all the difference. If you have these things in place, there is every reason to remain extremely optimistic about the present, and your future.

The Value of Optimism

People say I'm a pragmatic optimist - with optimism always in the forefront. I believe that being optimistic has real and tangible benefits on many levels.

Having an optimistic mindset not only helps you feel better mentally on a daily basis, but has obvious health benefits also. You are more in love with life, are looking forward to the future and are less likely to get sick; all of which help propel an upward cycle in your life. When you are confident and happy, you attract more of that into your life. You also attract more of the people you want in your life. Successful people with a good outlook and energy, who also want to be around you. That can be self-fulfilling on a personal level, and certainly when it comes to work, business, and investments. Think about it. If you stumbled on an event where Warren Buffett and Richard Branson were hanging out, are they more likely to invite you over, ask you to stay around for dinner, and freely share their investment strategies if you are walking around miserable, or if you are confident and exuding optimism?

Personal finances, businesses, investments, and entire markets and economies rise and fall on the presence of optimism, or lack thereof. It's a fact. When people act out of fear, pessimism, and a mindset of scarcity they tend to manage their finances, businesses, and investments less profitably. They pull back where they should be investing more. If an investment plummets 50%, and then you sell, guess what; you just created that loss. A loss that may not have been incurred if you rode out the dip. When the media starts hyping up the next surge, hotspot, or predicting the next crash, guess what happens? People are flocking in, or are selling out. Never mind that it often makes no rational sense.

Reality Check

There is a good chance many who are reading this right now are saying. "Well, what about reality?" You have to be realistic." You are absolutely right!

Being optimistic doesn't have to mean putting the blinders on, speculating with your money, or ignoring obvious financial and investment trends and changes. It is healthy to be realistic. At the same time though, you don't have to let that reality get you down, or dampen your optimism. It is about choosing a positive mindset. No matter what.

A good part of it is also about getting the right perception and context. In other words, don't panic and let your emotions get the better of you. Keep things in perspective. Maintain clarity and focus on "What do I need to do next?" "What is the best action I can take to create the best possible outcome?" Imagine a boxer in a ring. It is almost 100% certain that his opponent is going to throw blows at him, some of which are going to land. Some might even sting a bit. What's the best strategy? To drop his hands, turn and run? Isn't it smarter, safer, and more profitable for that boxer to keep his hands up in a guard position, and to make strategic footwork and striking moves, head on against his opponent? Isn't that far more likely to deliver a more positive outcome? Life and investing are a lot like that. You know some blows are going to come. If you are optimistic and prepared though, the chances of you taking blows are smaller while the chances you will win are 100x greater. You might wind up with a bruise now and again, but those will go away. Taking home a big pot of winnings, though, can last.

Identifying the Challenges
Being prepared and knowing what you are up against are key to a winning strategy and having justifiable optimism.

When fighters are coming up for a bout, or football teams are training, a big part of their time and their coaches' time is spent analyzing the competition. They are watching tape after tape, they have their eyes out on the data and the media, and are getting all the historical intel they can. The best coaches and players are not those that just sit on the sidelines their entire career, and watch everyone else getting results and having fun. They are actually the ones who get good at anticipating what plays, strikes, and strategies their opponents are likely to deploy in the upcoming games. In the case of football especially, coaches are thinking beyond the next game, beyond the season, and ahead to future years, and their overall career. They are looking at how to protect the players they have (capital), so they can be put on the field or traded (invested) for the next opportunity at the championship, next season (life stage), and beyond (succession and hall of fame).

Being confident in your pragmatic optimism, know that your financial future starts with identifying the potential challenges ahead. This may include changes in the markets, time off for injuries, the need to learn new things to be able to perform at a higher level, the need to have a well-rounded game (offense and defense), the need for finding a great coach and some form of leverage, and the commitment to consistently get out on the field, rain, shine, sleet or snow, whether there are bulls or bears on the field.

It's okay to acknowledge the challenges. In fact, it is far more helpful if you do. You can use the space at the back of this book to write down some of your top fears or expected challenges now. Follow that with three to five things you can do to prepare for them. It will be great to look back on these years down the road. Or even for your heirs to look at them one day and say "wow, they went ahead and took on these challenges, threw themselves into learning and thinking, and invested instead of cowering, and I can do it too!"

Overcoming the Issues
Knowledge and foresight are clearly two of the most important factors in overcoming challenges. As is maintaining a positive, but objective perspective, and being able to make decisions despite the distractions and perceived intensity of the moment. As an investor, there is a lot you can do to learn and prepare yourself. There is also a lot we can learn and benefit from good coaches and advisors.

Much can also be done to build in stamina, sustainability, flexibility, and strength, to get us through. These will also increase our chances of success, and thereby boost the levels we will be able to engage at and enjoy later on.

Successful investors win and achieve outsized success because they do not get hung up on the perceived challenges. When looking at their dream cars, homes, and yachts, or investment opportunities, they don't say "I can't afford it;" instead they think "how can I afford it?" Practice that next time you run into something really big you desire, or want to achieve. It will help develop your strategic thinking, and create a positive habit that can be used from starting a portfolio to navigating market changes and overcoming challenges later on.

Sometimes this will require:
- Learning new things
- Focus
- Determination
- Being flexible
- Strategic planning
- Diversifying and using multiple strategies at once

Commitment and practice makes a big difference too. If you have a good, well-rounded plan and portfolio, and stick with your vision, you'll get there. Sometimes it takes a little courage, but you can make it.

Teams
Teams are a powerful tool in maintaining the right mindset and championing challenges.

You simply can't know and do everything yourself all the time. Nor do you want to. At some point, you certainly want your investments to pay for your lifestyle and let you enjoy life. You may be a 'deal junkie' like me, and thrive on helping others and in making new investments. However, there is a big difference in having to do it, and doing it because you love doing it. It is about having the choice. The earlier you can gain that freedom the better, as you never know when you'll need it.

There are a number of benefits to having a team, including:
- Research and market intelligence
- Managing investments
- Accountability
- Expert insights and feedback
- Being surrounded by positivity
- Being connected to new opportunities
- Time leverage

These people can show up in a variety of ways, including:
- In-house employees
- Independent contractors and remote assistants
- Vendors
- Outsourced freelancers
- Professional advisors
- Peer support
- Coaches and mentors

Look at the most successful investors and wealthy members of Forbes' richest lists and you'll find they have the biggest teams. Some are hired, some are partners and others are advisors or friends.

They can often see challenges before you do, and can spot opportunities and solutions you do not see from your point of view. Then they can put them into action for you.

I am incredibly grateful for my teams. For everyone from my editors to office staff to freelance designers, software vendors, realtors, accountants, attorneys, mentors, and all the rest, including the investors on the journey with us.

However, it is also vitally important to get the right team in place. And honestly, this can take time. You have to be willing to take chances on people. You can do all the research, screening, resume reading, interviewing and personality tests in the world, but may still not nail the right fit.   Be prepared to hire, re-clarify your expectations, let people go, and replace as needed. Once you get a team that really gels and is on their game, don't let them go.

I find the most important components of the hiring process to be core values and energy. If prospects have these in common with you, you can teach them just about anything else. Without shared values, it isn't going to end well. If they don't bring good energy to you, your office and team, or interactions with your clients and vendors, that is going to drain you and your entire company. It'll get very expensive, very quickly.

Of course, even once you have your A-Team in place, things don't always go perfectly. You may be expanding into new things, and you may not have a system for everything you encounter in advance. We experienced just that when we leaped into the top end of the luxury market with million dollar house flips. We tried to be loyal to the local real estate agent who had really done an awesome job in moving our inventory in the past. It was just a little out of his league and he didn't have the buyer database that was the best match for the properties. That meant losing over 60 days of holding time due to one of the buyers falling out of the deal. We ended up flipping the listing to another luxury agent.

In addition, we hold weekly meetings and try to keep any slip ups transparent, without beating anyone up or breaking their spirit. These meetings are learning and problem solving sessions. Instead of harping on the losses, we lick our wounds, analyze what we could have done better in the scenario, and create a new process so that it never happens again. Then mitigate that risk and keep pushing forward.

Managing & Maintaining Your Optimism

Optimism isn't something you can just set and forget. Some may be more naturally optimistic than others, though there is a lot you can do to maintain and keep your optimism up too. A study of twins covered by Science Direct shows that only about 25% of optimism is inherited[2]. The rest is up to individuals and the environments they put themselves in.

If you've ever been to a Tony Robbins style motivational event you know that you can really get pumped up. You walk out of there high on life and optimism about the future. You may make some big goals or begin some bold changes, and want to rave about it to everyone you know and meet. For most that wears off pretty quickly though. Then things start to slide.

---

[2] https://www.psychologytoday.com/blog/the-science-behind-behavior/201608/simple-exercise-boost-optimism-and-improve-health

It takes being intentional to maintain a high life of optimism and results. Diet and exercise can have a great impact on your mindset, performance and levels of optimism. If you know any marine snipers they'll tell you they have to be incredibly meticulous about their diet, as everything they put in their bodies can impact their perspective. Research by Harvard, the University of Wisconsin, and University of Warwick, suggest that eating foods high in vitamin E and beta-carotene, such as carrots and spinach, can lead to more positivity. Exercise, health, and optimism levels are also linked. Interestingly though, Psychology Today says the best 'exercise' for boosting optimism is practicing visualization.

Many outstanding leaders and motivational experts also state that they don't watch the news. They recognize that optimism and performance is just as much about putting in the good as blocking out the negative. So instead, they put good books, podcasts, and music into their minds.

Who you hang out with is a big factor as well. I know I certainly had to make some adjustments to who I hung out, and did business with too. Spend your time with those who energize and lift you up, have an optimistic outlook, and want you to succeed too. That may mean hiring different people in your office and getting different vendors and advisors. It may also mean spending more time at the gym instead of at the local bar where most spend their time commiserating about how tough life is, and choosing your lunch and dinner companions more wisely. There are even a wide variety of optimist groups. There is the League of Pragmatic Optimists, Optimist International groups who work to inspire optimism in our youth, and a variety of chapters and groups on Facebook and in cities all around the country and world. Now there are even a variety of apps for boosting and maintaining optimism for both android and Apple devices. This includes Positive Thinking and ThinkUp for positive affirmations, as well as the Positive Activity Jackpot which gives users enjoyable activities to engage in so they stay in a good frame of mind. This is based on pleasant event scheduling (PES), a type of behavioral therapy which can be used to beat depression and avoid downward spirals according to the University of Michigan. It has been used for seniors, cancer patients, and may even benefit those with PTSD. So, no matter what you are going through, there are tools out there to help you get and stay in a successful frame of mind. If you ever find you really struggle here I recommend talking to or reading the biographies of those who have overcome incredible odds and challenges, from multiple time cancer survivors and heroes who are still amazingly grateful and bullish optimists, to those who have climbed from great poverty to being some of our most well-known wealthy leaders that live to inspire and help others. It can really put things in perspective for you.

Perhaps most interesting is Scott H. Young's perspective on pragmatic optimism and how your fear and doubts can allow you to succeed[3]. He is big on testing, (like Shark Tank investor Barbara Corcoran) and believes just getting started and experimenting is the best way forward. Being willing to learn and being okay with small failures along the way changes your perspective, kicks the fear element to the curb, and increases the potential for success. He uses reframing to go from "is it possible for me to do this?" to asking, "how can I improve my approach to make it possible?"

---

[3] https://www.scotthyoung.com/blog/2010/03/24/pragmatic-optimism-how-your-fears-and-doubts-can-allow-you-to-succeed/

ScienceDirect research on this shows that those with a high level of risk aversion are more demanding about wealth redistribution[4]. The more they shy away from any calculated risks, the more they just want to take from others who have put in the work and made the effort and the investments. Perhaps reversing that and being willing to take on small calculated experiments in investing will put more people in a position where they don't need to rely on the finances and hard work of others.

The most powerful thing you can do in the quest to stay out of the quicksand of self-pity is to focus on others. Go watch some vets who have lost limbs crush it in the gym or complete a marathon. It'll certainly blow away your excuses for not being able to get active. Walk through the most distressed neighborhoods in your town. See how many homeless people and families there are. See the seniors who can't keep up with their homes any more. Listen to the workers in the store with their children trying to explain to them why they can't afford that candy, despite how much time mom and dad have spent away from home working hard. These are people who could really use your help. And you can provide it by helping to change the dynamics of the neighborhood, supporting good employers and jobs, and being a good banker and note holder or landlord. Focus on helping others, and you won't have time to get stuck in other thoughts.

Optimism is ultimately a choice, but it certainly helps when you

---

4

http://www.sciencedirect.com/science/article/pii/S0047272717301019
?dgcid=raven_sd_aip_email

create healthy habits and routines. Surround yourself with optimistic people to gain new perspectives, be willing to try things, and maintain and manage your mindset.

Chapter 6:
The Truth About Real Estate

Real estate is undeniably one of the best options for investing. Yet, there are many ways to invest in real estate. That means busting through common myths that hold the masses back, and knowing your different options and strategies.

Your Home is Not an Investment

Top analysts say that most individuals and families are underexposed to real estate as an investment. Many own homes, but they may not have true real estate investments within their portfolio. Unless you really use smart strategies for your own residence, it can just be a big liability. That's why personal residences are not counted in net worth calculations or for qualifying as an accredited investor.

There are many benefits of homeownership, as it can provide stability and a foundation for many other things in life. Data from the National Association of Realtors even ties homeownership to better school performance and lower juvenile delinquency issues. In the long-term, children of homeowners are believed to become higher earners than their renter counterparts. Then there are the benefits of locking in predictable housing payments, lower living costs, and avoiding being held ransom by landlords and escalating rents.

However, for most, a residence is still just a liability, because it costs them money every month. This is especially true in today's mainstream consumer society which trends toward overspending and overleveraging.

There are ways to purchase and use a home as an investment. I personally have targeted my residences as an investment. There are a number of ways to do this. A great choice for a first home is a small 1-4 unit multifamily property. Home buyers can still qualify to use high LTV FHA, VA, USDA, and other loans on these properties. That means low down payments and lower interest rates than for those with conventional loans. They also provide an immediate source of income. For example, if you buy a triplex, you can live in one unit, and rent out the other two. That income can help you qualify for a home loan, and may even pay for your entire housing payments, and then some. If you are getting paid to buy and live there – that's an investment! Even if it doesn't cover your entire payment, it still provides a cushion in case you come up short one month.

PRO TIP: Some people rush to pay off their homes and desire to keep them 'free and clear' of financial obligations. I'd advise against this. First, it is important to note that your home is never really free and clear. You'll always have insurance and tax payments. Probably utilities and maybe association fees too. Secondly, having all that equity there makes you a big flashing target for scammers. There are thousands of criminals out there whose full-time job is to find people with equity that they can sue or run into on the road, and hit them with frivolous or malicious lawsuits. All that equity can be up for grabs in those scenarios, and they are far more common than you think[5]. I

---

[5] http://mullhoferlaw.com/frivolous-ada-lawsuits-filed-california-business-owners/

recommend at least taking out a home equity line of credit so that you can protect your home equity fast. You may also want to leverage your equity and use it to expand and invest. If you can borrow at 4% interest on your home, and reinvest it at 8%, that's a savvy financial move. Many will find that this is one of their best ways to start building up the capital to invest.

Buy Smart

Another part of this equation is simply to buy smart. The vast majority get hung up on trying to buy the perfect dream home right out of the gate. That's not usually realistic. Others far overextend themselves for it, and then just bury themselves up to the neck in debt for years, causing them to have to put off investing. This is incredibly counterproductive on many levels. Some people have woken up to this, and have been able to sell their oversized homes, downsize, and use the financial surplus they create to invest in real estate.

Look for value. If you are in the market to purchase a residence, look at it from an investment perspective. If it can't provide you income via an extra unit, or Airbnb, can you find a real deal, which you can walk into with some equity right away? Can you buy something for under market value? If you look hard and consistently you may be surprised at how great a deal you can get.

It helps if you really get a sound, big picture perspective too. Know what you can and can't fix. Avoid getting hung up on 'the pink carpet issue'. Too many first time home buyers go out there and start looking for their forever home. They think it has to be perfect right away, and fit into their budget. That's a combo which is almost impossible to find. Differentiate between what you can and can't fix. If you are buying a $300,000 home, don't blow off a great deal because the carpet in the third bedroom is pink. You can replace that for a few hundred dollars. You can't however, change the location, or the construction material, or lot size. At least not as easily.

It's also important to realize that you probably won't stay there forever. Americans typically move around every 5 years. If you stayed for 10 or 15 years, that would seem extreme and even more so given the increasingly mobile and location independent world we live in. So it doesn't have to be perfect. It doesn't have to work for your family expansion plans for the next few decades. Use it as a tool to build some capital, and use that money to level up. Between the weather, changing markets, life changes, changes in taste and in the neighborhood, and evolving housing needs, that first home may not last forever, or be desirable to you for the long term.

One friend of mine and his father have really nailed this and are doing live-in flips. In other words, they buy a home, move in, fix it up, and sell it for a handsome profit. Then they do it again. They might move a couple times a year, but it works for them, and they are making great money.

The Need for Diversification

Another reason to invest in real estate outside of your residence is for diversification. At least if you want to preserve what you have, build more wealth, while creating sustainable passive income streams.

Diversification can also offer a form of 'insurance'. A well- diversified portfolio will keep you covered when specific assets or niches falter or fail to provide the desired growth and income. If you have just one property and that neighborhood dips in value or vacancies go up, or a hurricane comes through, you are not going to have a fun year. If you have 10 properties in 10 different locations and niches, it would be rare for them all to be affected at the same time. Some will probably begin out performing, when the others slow down.

Many stock brokers recommend their clients engage in broad diversification. They suggest they invest in a wide variety of funds, and funds of funds. They do this, as they'll admit, because they really have no idea what is going to work. They don't really know what is going to go up or down, or when. Unfortunately, that slows any potential for growth enormously, and since it's all stocks, they can suffer from the same volatility at the same time. It's kind of like putting your money on almost every number on the roulette wheel on one throw. Plus, it can mean numerous layers of fees.

That is completely different than proactive strategic diversification. The type of strategic diversification I am talking about is more like a championship football team. If you had the chance to pick your own fantasy team, what would it look like? You'd probably have a couple of great coaches. You'd have a defense and offense. You'd have a quarterback, wide receivers, running backs, and linebackers. If you owned the team you'd want the best coaches you could find to manage the team, evaluate, select the right players, and what moves they'll make. Some of their roles are specifically to protect your goal. Others' missions and purpose are just to run the ball and get it to the end zone. Some plays are about getting the next few feet down the field. Others are about throwing or kicking the ball, or carrying it to the end of the field. You'll probably even have a B team on the bench to step in, in case of an injury. You can't win if you only have defense. If you only have an offensive line you'll probably be at a disadvantage when it comes to defense. Just like in football, you need a well-rounded strategic team and portfolio.

The Truth about DIY Investing

Many self-appointed real estate gurus have popped up in the past few years, who sell the dream of making millions from real estate, fast and easy. The majority, of course, are making the bulk of their money from charging for courses or acting on TV, rather than actually doing real estate investing themselves. These people are just cashing in on selling the idea, without giving a ton of value, and often make things worse for individual investors by selling them on the wrong strategies, and making it sound easier than it really is. Real estate investing can be simple, with the right strategy, but too frequently these students are sent on numerous endless wild goose chases, or sabotage their real goals by trying to do too much themselves.

You can jump right in and invest all by yourself. It is vital though, to ensure that your strategy and tactics are really able to deliver on the results you really want. And you also want to assess fairly accurately what it will take.

Common challenges with this DIY approach include:
- Limited ability to scale
- Huge time demands (more than a full-time job)
- Limited freedom to take vacations or time away

- Big investments required in marketing
- Lots of trial and error
- Difficulty in diversification

Take flipping houses for example. As a solo investor, you are often exposed to big risks at the beginning. Each deal can take a lot of capital, a lot of marketing mastery, and one blunder can bankrupt you.

As a do it yourself rental property landlord, you can also find yourself thrown into a massive job. Just a few units can be more than a full time job for one person. You face physical risks collecting rents, legal risks dealing with tenants, and can find it virtually impossible to take time off, as you always need to be on hand to take tenant calls and make repairs 24/7, 365 days per year.

On the other hand, going DIY might be a great fit for you, and is doable. It can also be far more fun and rewarding than any other job. You just need to know what is truly involved and what it will require of you. Others may find more automated strategies a better fit for their lifestyle and goals.

It's All About the Management

Regardless of whether you go the DIY route with your real estate investing, or you invest through a broker or a fund, it is really all about the management and execution.

The most lucrative looking investment opportunities can wind up terrible failures due to poor management. Yet, even mediocre investments, or those that scare many off can be immensely profitable with great management.

It's about excellent management when it comes to evaluating and negotiating opportunities, having smooth closings, and timing exits well. And the daily asset management, is just as important. That means keeping up occupancy rates, maximizing income, maintenance, managing contractors, adding value, managing the books, customer service, and a lot more.

It takes years of real in-depth experience, access to great data, and a highly effective team across all of these areas to really operate and manage properties to their full potential. Fortunately, there are two factors which are making this easier and more profitable; the new sharing economy or 'democratization' of real estate and investments, and technology.

The Sharing Economy

There has been a massive push to 'democratize' industry and investing in recent years. Some call this 'The Sharing Economy'. In many ways it is lowering barriers to entry, increasing efficiency, lowering risk, and improving profitability.

Some of the most notable examples of this that come to mind are Uber for transport, Amazon in retail, Airbnb for travel, Facebook for content, and Twitter for news.

This is also happening in the real estate and investment worlds. In the wake of 2008, banks and big financial institutions have lost a lot of their credibility, trust, and value. Individuals have woken up to the fact that with the help of technology they can do a lot more by themselves and with each other too.

The biggest banks and institutions have been found to continually get caught up in massive fraud, all while delivering lower returns, and worse service at higher costs. Putting money on deposit with them, investing with them, borrowing from them, and even just giving them your personal information has proven to be incredibly risky, dangerous, and costly. They were once the go-to default method of storing and growing wealth. They'd borrow your capital, invest it carefully, and give you a share of the profits. That share has gotten pretty small, sometimes even negative when factoring inflation in. Other times it is about all of the bloated and inefficient layers of administration and fees. Or it can just be terrible management choices in terms of service.

At the same time, new regulation changes like the JOBS Act, new technology, and awareness of alternatives has been empowering individuals to take back control of their finances and financial futures with new options.

Three of the ways this is showing up are:
1.   Private lending
2.   Direct investment
3.   Private partnerships

Some individuals are cutting out the banks by copying their investment tactics and making loans to real estate investors. Instead of giving their money to the bank to make loans, and having them eat up 70% or more of the returns, you can do it yourself or through other platforms, and generate high single digit and even double digit returns, while having better transparency about what you are investing in.

In addition to new loans, individual investors can also invest directly in existing mortgage notes, in income properties, or participate in house flipping. Again, this can eliminate a lot of fluff fees and inefficiencies, provide more clarity on the real collateral, and has the potential for far larger net returns.

Many individuals don't want to do this all alone though, and they shouldn't. Having partners helps to lower and spread risks, leverage expertise and time, and accelerate and improve the ability to scale and diversify investments. This can be done through private partnerships, joint family offices, crowdfunding, private funds, and within self-directed IRAs and 401ks.

AI & Tech in Investing
From new iPhones, to virtual reality goggles, to drones, self-driving cars, smart home tech, and big data, we've come a long way with technology in just a few years. And it keeps speeding up.

This hasn't just helped spawn new apps and websites for investing through, but in many ways is making real estate investing safer, more convenient, and more profitable.

Speed is a big game changer. Now fund managers can evaluate thousands of potential investments in less time than it used to take to research a single asset. Investors can now act more quickly via the web too, enabling them to take advantage while prices are good. Plus, we can now invest across the whole map, just as easily as investing next door. That means being able to benefit from the best possible spreads, the safest and the most likely to grow destinations anywhere, from anywhere. You can take a year off to travel the Caribbean or Southeast Asia, and never miss an opportunity on notes, houses, or multifamily investments in New Jersey.

These improved options, access, and efficiencies are all making investing more profitable.

Never before have we enjoyed such access to information and knowledge either. Now, with just a couple of clicks, there is endless data, graphs on real estate and economic trends and cycles, and deep due diligence can be performed on individual properties and debt instruments. You can pull 50 plus data points on a single property online with good tools and systems, and view all the metrics going on in the local economy, and even a lot of what is happening behind the scenes at financial institutions' books.

While overall this is reducing potential risks in investing, it has also created some new challenges of its own. It's great that we can show exactly what we are doing via HD video, providing transparency and accountability with detailed reports, and 24/7 monitoring of investments. Yet, the ease of publishing on the internet, and desperateness of many sites and businesses to publish and attract readers means there is enormous volumes of junk, low quality information and fake news. Now one of the most important roles, according to billionaire investor Mark Cuban, is having experts not for generating this information, but to decipher it. Individual investors stand to benefit a lot from all of this technology and data, but still need hyper-experienced humans to accurately decipher the data and translate what it really means.

Chapter 7:
An Introduction to Notes

Note investing has emerged as a highly attractive way to invest in financial instruments and the real estate market.

Discovering Note Investing

It was just after the 2008 financial crisis and I was desperately trying to help large numbers of hurting homeowners. I had been flipping houses, acquiring rentals, and working with distressed property owners to obtain short sales. Sadly, the banks and servicers were a mess. They couldn't get things done, and often wouldn't do the things they could. That's when my son suggested I become the bank. That we step up and take over those loans, and become the lender, so that we could actually really give people the help they needed. Plus, why should those banks keep on taking people's deposits and profiting from them, when they had been found to be some of the biggest culprits in what was the largest fraud in the history of our planet? Don't homeowners and individual savers and investors deserve someone better to serve them?

And that's exactly what we did. We became the 'bank'. I learned everything there was to know about mortgages and mortgage notes and servicing. We began buying homeowners' debts from the big banks, lenders, servicers, and special asset managers. We took on the loans that they weren't getting paid on. We mastered doing this efficiently while acquiring the notes at great discounts. We were helping the employees at those institutions and the economy from an even worse fate. Then we were helping the borrowers, by giving them a new lender who they could trust, and who actually wanted to help and was efficient enough to do so. Sometimes we even sat down with them one-on-one and helped them figure out their bills and personal finances, and even found them new jobs. We modified their loans and provided payment plans that they could really afford, and wouldn't have to spend more sleepless nights freaking out about keeping a roof over their kids' and parents' heads. A few just couldn't make it, or no longer wanted their homes. In those cases we worked to make it as easy and painless as possible to gain a fresh new start. We've made a lot of money in the process, but looking back it's the stories that are really priceless. Having that level of impact on a person or family, and their next generation has no price tag. You never know what child is going to grow up to be the next real world changer for the better and all because you helped them reach their full potential. In the process those who partnered with us and invested with us in these efforts enjoyed making some of the greatest returns of their lives. It became a true win-win-win. This remains one of my favorite methods of investing. I think it will always play an important role in my portfolio, and in the family estate I expect my sons, and their sons will manage.

The Concept

The concept of note investing is relatively simple.

As an investor you can buy existing mortgage loans from banks, mortgage lenders, credit unions, the government, and even other private investors.

You can buy these loans at a discount. Either at a discount from the remaining payments, or the unpaid principal balance (UPB).

This is much like big institutions, hedge and pension funds, and Wall Street have done for years.

As the new owner of these loan notes, which are secured by real estate (homes, condos, multifamily apartments, land and commercial properties) you have several options. You can simply collect the payments as a passive investment if the loans are performing. You can resell the notes to other investors. Modification agreements or refinances can be worked out with borrowers to get them back on track. Short sales can be granted to recoup capital and profits faster. Or you can take over the property and flip or rent it. Properties can even be sold on lease options or with wrap around mortgages in markets where it is needed to maximize sales prices and profit margins when mortgage lending is tight. All while giving individuals, couples and families the great opportunity of becoming homeowners. Sometimes you may even mix it up with a variety of these strategies.

As with all things in life the note market is always changing. Levels of access to deal flow, regulation, licensing and competition for different types and qualities of mortgage paper will always be shifting. With experience, you'll come to notice that as one of these areas over-performs, the others may become less of a focus for certain periods.

At NNG, we keep masses of historical and current data. We get access to data that most investors and note buyers don't even know is available. For example, even though some have complained that deals are scarcer and discounts much smaller in recent years, we've been tracking all the tangible data on trades being made out there.

We find out what the big trades sold for and keep a record of it. We also attend events and find out more about what assets are trading for in the trenches. Especially on the NPL (non-performing loan) and RPL (re-performing loan) side. We track data from loans we've sold. These three methods help us to keep our pulse on the market, and be more dialed in than most.

That gives us great negotiating power and wisdom in making acquisitions. For example, during late 2018, when most investors said they were struggling to find deals, we were still finding notes for as low as 40% to 85% for first mortgages. Even in non-judicial states where notes are commonly trading at par, there is great room for profit. You might buy a note for the unpaid principal balance of $50k. Yet, the borrower's actual payoff might be $85k, with plenty of equity on top of that. No matter what business you are in, that's a nice profit margin.

If you can buy in bulk as a fund, you can get much better deals, with lower risk and more upside as well. I've looked at tapes with individual paper assets available for 24 cents on the dollar. Then I found we can negotiate buying the whole pool or tape with a blended average of just 18 cents on the dollar.

For a more in-depth understanding of notes and what to look for in note investments, get a copy of Turning Distress into Success from Amazon.

Types of Notes

There are a many different types of notes for investors to choose from.

Residential Mortgage Notes
These are mortgage loans secured by residential property. These include single family homes, condos, townhomes, manufactured homes, co-ops, and small 2-4 unit multifamily properties. They may be owner occupied, second homes, vacation homes, investments, or vacant.

Commercial Mortgage Notes
These are loans on commercial properties. They may include 5 plus unit multifamily apartment buildings, offices, retail malls and shopping plazas, gas stations, churches, hospitals, lots and acreage, and industrial property. These are typically larger loans, and can be faster to foreclose on if needed.

Construction Loans
These are an often overlooked pocket of the market which can be abounding in deals. They consist of loans made to build or renovate properties. These commercial and residential properties, and even entire buildings and developments can be in various stages of work, from basic infrastructure to complete.

Performing Loan Notes
Performing loans are those on which borrowers have been paying on time, and are on track. They also trade for the lowest returns, and least discounts.

Non-Performing Loans
Non-performing loans are those on which borrowers are behind. This could be anywhere from 90 days late and above, to those already in the foreclosure process. These offer the biggest discounts and most profit potential.

Re-performing Loans

These are loans where the payment history isn't perfect. At some point the borrowers fell behind, but are now on track and are paying again. These can offer a great blend of both discounts and performance.

First Mortgages

This is your standard first position mortgage. It is the superior lien on a piece of property. It needs to be paid off and satisfied before any other loan. Some investors like that comfort, but the spreads are typically far thinner than on other loans.

Second Mortgages

Seconds, HELOCs, lines of credit, and even third mortgages can really fall into this category. They usually offer the best returns.

Other Types of Debt

Debt investing isn't limited to mortgage loans either. Debt investors can also engage in many other varieties, including credit card debts, business loans, auto loans, tax liens, collections and judgments.

Principles of Smart Note Investment

Investing in notes is all about achieving an asymmetric risk to reward ratio when you buy.

You are looking for incredible upside potential. With performing notes you are buying into a current income stream, with the added payment security. With non-performing notes you are striving for a deep discount that gives you great security just in case you can't work it out with the borrower. Always look to strike win-win solutions for all involved, but risks need to be priced in ahead of time.

With notes, having multiple exit strategies plays a major role in creating winning scenarios all around. Still, you need to know what those strategies are. Smart investors evaluate the different exits upfront, and make sure their price facilitates multiple possible exits. For example, will you be able to work out the note and hold it? Sell the note and get a cash payment? Take over the property and flip or rent it?

One of the most important make or break factors in investing in notes or REOs is being realistic about how you can get your hands on them. The common misconception is that you can just walk into a local bank branch, cold call the bank manager or loan servicer's 800 number, send a postcard, or cold email and pick up individual assets at awesome discounts, fast.

This industry is in constant flux. There was a time when even major banks were so hammered with distressed property that you could find amateur house flyers posted in your local branch. Yet, at the time of writing this book, things have changed quite a bit. There really are no more $100k buys. You can expect to spend at least $2M to even get to talk to someone. Banks are also far more reluctant to release tapes of inventory. They've come under fire for selling to the wrong types of buyers. They have more responsibility to try and sell non-performing notes to note buyers who will make a good faith effort to work things out with the borrowers instead of just trying to force foreclosure to scoop the properties. When it comes to REOs, they also need to be wary of selling to those who are going to leave homes abandoned for extended periods of time or fail to pay property taxes.

The bottom line is that is this has become or returned to more of a relationship business. To buy good notes and REOs at good prices, efficiently, you have to connect and build great relationships with the right contacts.

Workouts are an important part of note investing. You've got to know your options, your legal boundaries, and smart processes for working notes out in a profitable and sustainable manner. Once that milestone is crossed then it is all about highly effective asset management to keep those notes performing well, and identifying the right time and method of exit.

In order to do so and to make intelligent note investments, you must be thorough in due diligence. The due diligence involved in mortgage notes is notably different than other types of real estate investment. You really have to pay attention to potential liens on the property, as well as chain of title. There can be tax liens, association liens, mechanics liens, utility liens, code enforcement liens, and you should also evaluate the homeowner.

It is important to know the real data too. In 2010 the banks realized they could make a lot more if they carefully throttled the market; if they controlled the flow of available properties that is. Meanwhile, it can appear there is little inventory out there. That causes novice investors and regular home buyers to frequently grossly overpay for assets, and make rash moves. There can be a huge difference in what the average individual or investor sees, and what is happening behind the scenes on the books of banks, lenders, and servicers. A lot of this information can be accessible to serious buyers, or if you know where to view these firms' accounting records.

Chapter 8:
Flipping Houses

Flipping houses can be highly profitable and exciting. How much it lives up to the expectations depends a lot on how you do it.

The Dream
The ideal of flipping houses has almost become more the American Dream than settling down for the long term and having a white picket fence.

'Reality' TV has made house flipping very trendy. Even many wealthy celebrities are doing it. Some are riding the coattails of the trend to bring their personal brand back and return to the spotlight, such as Ellen and even Vanilla Ice!

The idea being sold is that you can get into real estate investing and make big money, fast and easy. Often, with the promise you can do it with no money, no credit, and no experience. That sells a lot of expensive courses. Sometimes it helps thrust individuals into a new career they love. Other times is seduces them into a highly stressful and costly string of life lessons.

You can make great money flipping houses. Quarterly data from RealtyTrac shows that average gross profit on a flip (defined as a house resold within 12 months) has often been between $45,000 and $65,000. In some areas gross profits have even exceed expectations. And that can just sound too good to be true, versus the miserable returns we have been trained to expect from big banks and other investments.

The draw is more than just about the big money though. Many are desperate for the time freedom and flexible schedule that flipping houses is advertised as. Reclaiming time can be absolutely priceless.

Then there are the fun and non-monetary rewards associated with real estate investing. It's a chance to do a different kind of work. Some find the physical part of renovating and beautifying houses very therapeutic. For others it is a chance to flex their art and design skills, or their creativity in coming up with solutions. Or the appeal can simply be in helping others, and supporting yourself while doing good.
Flipping houses can deliver on all of these things. Yet, it is important to remain realistic while you are flexing your optimism.

The Reality

The dream has worked out for many investors. They've begun making incredible incomes, enjoying unbelievable amounts of flexible time, and are having a blast at the same time. Others have rushed in however, running only on the vapor of the dream without having educated themselves, and have hit the wall of reality pretty hard.

The quick clips of house flipping on TV are just the highlight reels. Not only can there be a lot more physical and mental work, but there is a lot more to the numbers too. The gross numbers shown on television often don't account for many of the expenses involved. Many of those deals would be in the negative if you really did all the math. You have to watch your net. It's about what you get to keep at the end of it all, and the ROI on your money, and time.

Some love the idea of wielding their artistic touch in renovating and decorating houses. Yet, few realize that the vast majority of major and common improvements lose money, not even returning what they cost.

Item	Cost for Mid-Range Improvement	% of Cost Recouped
Bathroom addition	$43,252	53.9%
Bathroom remodel	$18,546	64.8%
Deck addition	$17,249	65.2%
Major kitchen remodel	$62,158	65.3%
Roofing replacement	$20,664	68.8%
Siding replacement	$14,518	76.4%

In our business, my rule is that every dollar in, needs to be able to generate at least $2 back. You've got to know the difference between doing this as a hobby or as a business. If you want to make money, you need to know a lot more than the average realtor.

You need to know what really adds tangible value you can bank on, how to manage contractors, the architect, and have relationships with vendors. What if a project requires $45,000 in sheetrock alone? On top of your repair budget? You'll need some slack or vendor credit too.

Even though common 'wisdom' says to "make your money when you buy," many don't even do that well. They speculate and gamble on what they hope the future will bring for property prices. That's not a strategy. While you can mitigate a lot of risk, and build in a lot of profit potential when you buy, you really don't realize that profit until you get the checks from the money coming back out. I side with Warren Buffett in that one way to do that is through income. If you can start getting income from rents or mortgage payments in 30 days, you are getting a return. However, your true net is only realized when you exit and tally it all up.

What Makes a Profitable Flip

A profitable flip relies on several factors, including:
- A good acquisition price
- Thorough due diligence
- Accurate repair estimates
- Expert contractor management
- Superior marketing to exit the property

Due diligence for flipping houses doesn't just rely on accurately assessing what you have. You also need to be skilled in assessing what you can do with it. You can never just rely on the listing realtor or the seller. And you can't rely on all of the public websites out there for statistics either. You have to dig deep and know how to assess values, and recognize the best way to position a property and resell it too.

There are ways you can invest in real estate and do most house flipping right online. Yet, knowing your market and what's really going on in the street is vital too. I still get out twice a week in person to go through the neighborhoods we are investing in, and to check out our properties in progress. It keeps contracting teams on their toes. Being on the field can also open your eyes to new opportunities, and help with spotting issues - as pictures don't always tell the whole story.

Then you have to know the best ways to position, market, and sell a property once the rehab is done. A lot of value is won or lost in this part of the game. You might include a key feature that gives it that wow factor for the best paying buyers, without having to blow your budget. This could involve positioning the property for hi-tech workers or a corporate housing, or through offering owner financing and creating new loans.

Smarter Ways to Participate

If you are really drawn to everything about hands-on house flipping, then it is definitely worth a try. If what you really want is just to enjoy the profits, or perhaps to have a hand in recycling distressed properties and helping the owners and communities involved, then there are other ways to participate.

Those who want to be active investors but who don't have the funds or desire to rehab can try real estate wholesaling, and become suppliers to flippers and landlords who need inventory.
Those with the funds to invest but who desire a more passive role while they remain free to get on with what they love most, have a couple of options. Partnerships are the most obvious. Put up the cash, let someone else to all the manual work, and split the profits. Private lending is also thrown around more frequently as an alternative. Both of these can work, though they can be more time intensive than anticipated. You still have to carefully source someone to work with, put the paperwork together right,

watch the legalities, and be on call in case they drop the ball.

Or you can invest in a real estate fund, which is the most passive way to invest. All the legal paperwork is handled for the investor. There tends to be a big team involved, and key persons are insured so there is never a worry of one individual failing to perform and impacting the investment. Plus, investments are far over-collateralized.

Rental Property Investing

Much of what we've covered on flipping houses also applies to income property investing. It's true for single family rental homes and multifamily apartment buildings.

You still need to buy right, do the due diligence, make the right calls on repairs and improvements, and choose the right exits. As with flipping, the way many are sold on rental property investing is not very accurate either. In reality, it's far more time consuming and expensive than expected and not as passive as many believe it is. DIY landlords are pretty much taking on a full time job that typically requires a whole team. Scaling a portfolio like that can get slow and cumbersome, especially when you are essentially on call for tenants 24 hours a day, 7 days a week, 365 days a year.

We are also in an era with thousands of new landlords, property management companies, and investment banks trying to capitalize on this nation of renters. It's often the blind leading the blind. There are millions of vacant homes and apartments in America, many of which are owned by investors who haven't mastered the leasing and tenant selection process. They are out of touch with the rental market where they are investing. Some set unrealistic criteria for tenant applicants, or just fail to be competitive. Then they are stuck with empty units, which are emptying their bank accounts each month.

To find the best yields you may have to invest out of your area or in areas where others are afraid to go. Everyone wants to own ultra-prime property in Manhattan, San Francisco and on Miami Beach, but those properties rarely offer good deals, reasonable entry prices, or above market yields. Wherever you invest make sure to possess local market knowledge, and savvy local property management. You need to know how that market is evolving, especially in terms of the tenant pool. It's no good demanding $100 in application fees for renters, 700 credit scores, and three of rent months upfront, if your competition is offering free rent deals and 90% of the tenant pool has 650 or less credit scores.

We love to give tenants an opportunity. The best strategies for keeping up occupancy rates, and keeping a balance have proven to be having a very systematic application evaluation process and tracking performance. We use Appfolio for screening, and make sure applicants haven't had an eviction in the last two years. We look at the whole picture, and specifically at the factors that predict rental performance. In addition, if we offer deals, we document it. Then we carefully track the performance of those leases. If they are working out, then we'll repeat the deals. If not, we shelf them.

This becomes important when trying to grow an income portfolio, and diversify into different areas. Again, you can do it yourself, partner up, or use a passive vehicle and strategy.

Chapter 9:

The Problem with Funds

Funds can be great, or not so great an investment.

The Problem with [Most] Real Estate Funds

Funds and similar structures can offer both great advantages, and disadvantages. There are many entities which can be lumped in with this term, even though they may be very different in structure and strategy.

These include:
- Sovereign funds
- Pension funds
- Partnerships
- Hedge funds
- Private equity funds
- REITs (Real Estate Investment Trusts)

There are two main potential issues with big funds. The first is that many people don't even really know why it is that they are investing in them in the first place, with the funds often simply being a default go-to within a brokerage or retirement account. Little effort is really made on many people's parts to figure out what they are actually investing in, what the fees are, and why.

The second is that a lot of big funds are simply too big. Management is too distant from the front lines - too insulated from what is happening in the streets and local marketplace. On top of it, the hefty and complex layers of admin and fees can just soak up the majority of the gains. At some point these funds can find it hard to efficiently allocate capital due to size, or revert from what helped them grow, and turn to ultra-conservative strategies with negligible returns. Look at some company pension funds, who are now desperately trying to buy out employees because they are not on track to deliver promised benefits. It almost sounds like the Social Security Administration.

Others may not be diversified, or can be diversified far too widely in many lines of business. There may be a place in your overall financial plan for all of these types of investments, but providing they are chosen intently, and in the right amounts. There are good funds. It's just a matter of finding those which are best for you, your goals, and your timeline.

What Makes a Great Fund

What should we be looking for in a fund?
If I was to invest in another fund this would be my checklist:

- Are producing results in line with my goals
- Are investing in line with my timeline
- Share my values
- Care about what they do
- Care about who they impact
- Offer personal interaction
- Have experienced management
- They know the game
- Are future proofed
- I can earn 7% or more annually on my investment

Investing Aligned with Your Goals
There are a variety of good investments, and even funds out

there. Not all will be in alignment with your personal goals and objectives though. If you are at a stage where you need to grow your wealth and portfolio, you really can't afford to be in a fund that is offering 4% returns before taxes because the inflation and taxes will destroy you. If this is money that you are investing for the long term, for a nest egg, for an estate plan or retirement, and you really can't afford to lose it, then you can't just gamble on the hope of striking it rich in a new tech startup either. The bottom line is that you need to know your wants and needs from this investment.

Your Timeline
Some funds may be positioned for great short term growth, but could be headed for trouble and big downturns in the mid to long term. Others may be targeting the very long term (100 years plus), but may not provide the returns, income and growth you need in the next 5 to 10 years.

Investing in Line with Your Values
Remember what's most important to you. Money is great, we all need it. Yet, we know it can't replace or make up for many other things. You definitely don't want to invest in something just for the money, only to sacrifice your more important priorities. For example, I really don't want to support anything which is going to make life worse for my kids in the future. What's the point in leaving them a few extra dollars if I contributed to making their environment toxic? Know your values and priorities.

Invest with People Who Care About What They Do
Are they running this fund, recommending it, or advertising it just because it is a job and they need the money? Or do they care about what they do? Do they care about doing quality work?

Invest with People Who Care About the People They Impact

As a business owner, fund manager, or investor you touch a lot of lives. You can take, take, take, and get, get, get for a little while, and do a lot of damage at the same time. Or you can add value, where others are leaving a big gap. A big part of the reason I began investing in mortgage notes was specifically to fill this void. Not everyone cares. At the end of the day though, it is simply math. Nonetheless, understand this - if you are out there burning people, and sowing a lot of problems, sooner or later, somehow, it is going to come back to you. Do you want to own shares in a ticking time bomb like that? It's not something I personally want to bet my finances or kids' financial future on.

Personal Service

Technology is awesome. You can now do just about anything with a couple clicks or sometimes by simply speaking a few words into your phone or smart home device. Such ease can even apply to investing, which is great. Yet, there are times when you want to speak to a real human. Even to be able to go meet someone face to face, or visit their office. It's nice to have both options.

Experienced Management

There are lots of aspiring investors and fund managers, many with stunning degrees. There is no substitute for experience though. There is an advantage to being on the front lines, and possessing the experience only time can provide, in order to plan ahead soundly. Too many simply haven't been around long enough to know what they don't know, and to know how to build sustainability into their enterprises.

Asset Managers That Know the Game

Stocks, financing, and even the real estate market is a big game.

At least for some. You can argue that the 2008 financial crises were the result of simple stupidity. Others might argue that it was all orchestrated. Whatever the case was then, as with previous stock market crashes, it is highly likely there will be other cases of pump and dump. Funds and investors just along for the ride may not see it. Or don't care. I'd rather be aware, and play them at their own game.

Future Proof
The future is tomorrow, next year, ten years, or 100 years from now. A solid real estate fund isn't just hot for a few years. It should be balanced and focused enough to deliver consistent results. That applies whether or not notes are still selling for pennies on the dollar, REOs are available in bulk, housing prices are up or down, and whether people are trending toward buying homes or renting apartments.

Starting Your Own Fund
Another option is to simply start your own fund.

For some it can be a profitable and logical play. Yet, it comes with a lot of responsibility, and typically a sizable investment.

I cover a lot of the details of setting up and launching your own fund in Turning Distress into Success. While some like to make it sound very simple to raise money under the new JOBS Act, you can still expect it to set you back six figures to successfully launch a profitable fund. There are substantial legal fees to deal with in order to get the paperwork filed correctly. Then there is the waiting on the SEC, and being able to master the marketing aspect or at least bring in a skilled marketing and customer service team. If you're not confident in raising at least a couple million right off the bat though, starting a fund may not be the best move yet.

Some savvy alternatives still exist, including:
- Working with, or organizing a multi-family office to invest in funds
- Starting a family trust or philanthropic trust to invest through
- Using your IRA or 401k to invest while retaining tax protections
- Referring clients and business to a fund if you are an influencer or professional
- Partnering with peers to invest in a fund, and meeting the minimums for access to superior investments

One of the big benefits of having your own fund is being able to build equity within your fund, brand, and company, which offers a compounded financial upside, on top of the returns, your stake, or any management fees (if you levy any). Thinking big and long could lead to your fund owning its own commercial properties and other assets, as well as the potential for being bought by an even larger fund. Or like Warren Buffett, you can use your fund to partner with other funds, companies, and financiers on even larger deals.

Investing Success in the New Era

Many describe this as a new era. Could it simply be though that we've awoken to some basic truths which have been hiding out there for many decades and centuries?

The truth is that nothing grows consistently and evenly, forever.

Not stocks, not gold, and not the economy, or even houses in NYC or LA, nor the spreads available on certain types of mortgage loan notes, or taxes.

Over the long term, real estate has definitely proven to go up, up, and up though. The graph below shows that, in addition to the varying image which details the changes in 30 year mortgage rates over the years.

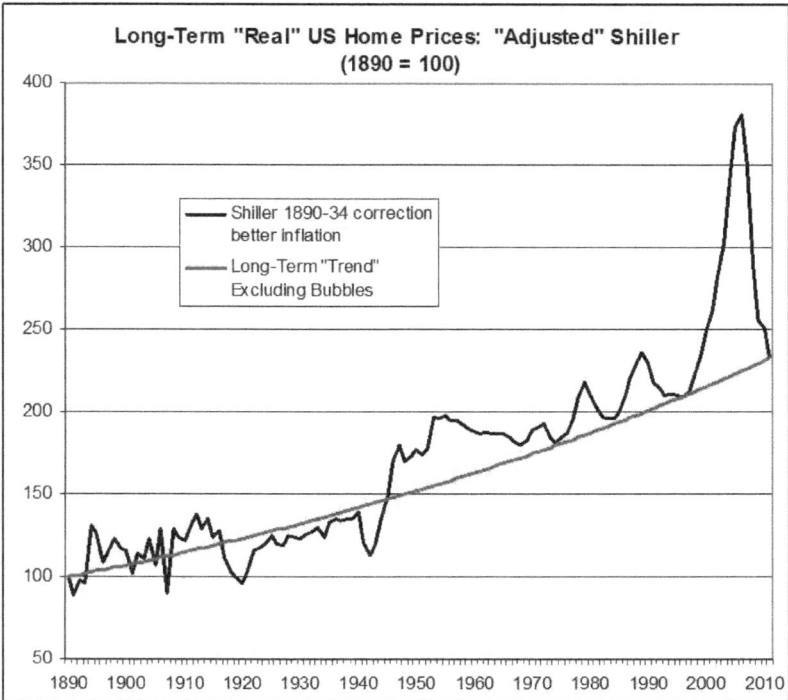

Long-Term "Real" US Home Prices: "Adjusted" Shiller (1890 = 100)

Legend:
- Shiller 1890-34 correction better inflation
- Long-Term "Trend" Excluding Bubbles

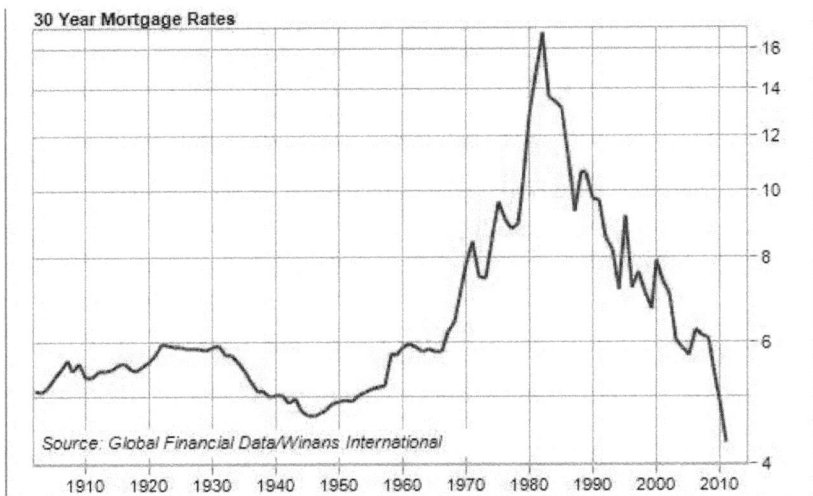

30 Year Mortgage Rates

Source: Global Financial Data/Winans International

You can't just look at the long term when investing though. You have to make good mid-term investments that don't bring on too much risk in the short term and maximize your long term potential.

So, you don't just sit in stocks while they are plummeting, while hoping to have another 7-14 years to bounce back to par before needing the money. You create a hybrid portfolio which provides protection from any downward trends, and which can consistently deliver income, regardless of exterior trends. This allows you to continue making leaps in wealth, in both good and bad years.

The Hybrid Approach

What we do to build in the best defense and greatest upside potential in our hybrid fund is to incorporate a variety of assets focused on the real estate and mortgage finance sectors.

We invest in:
- First mortgages
- Second mortgages
- Performing notes
- Non-performing notes
- Renovating and reselling real estate
- Acquiring buy and hold real estate

The first thing we do with a new fund is to achieve arbitrage and immediate positive cash with performing mortgage notes. Thereby, we instantly create spreads and passive income, forming a great foundation for the fund and its investors. With income coming in, this turns a solid profit for investors right away.

Then we add in discounted notes and real estate, which create equity in the fund, and a solid position that defends it from any potential future market dips. For example, if we are acquiring notes at pennies on the dollar, or foreclosed assets at 60% of value, and the market drops 10% in a year, we've still created value and equity. If desired, those assets can be liquidated for a profit as well.

Then we renovate income producing properties in a buy and hold strategy, which continues producing cash flow and positive yields, even if the value of real estate fluctuates. Typically, with a foreclosure crisis, more people are forced to rent. That's great for landlords.

We take other distressed properties, which are acquired at discounts, and renovate and resell them to put lump sums of profit into the fund. This can be done in any phase of the market, and spurs growth, even if the only mortgage notes coming available have low rates, or rents are not growing quickly.

This, we believe and have experienced, provides ongoing strength and growth to the fund.

Chapter 10:
Never Stop Innovating

What's Next?

Consistently successful CEOs, entrepreneurs, fund managers, and individual investors all have one thing in common. They are always asking, "what's next?"

We simply cannot stay stuck on the status quo. If we did, we would have an even worse housing shortage in America. We would not have the economy and luxurious lifestyle we experience today (and that applies to at least 90% of those living in the US). We wouldn't be making progress in cleaning up and preserving our environment, and we wouldn't be living nearly as long, or leaving much to our children. We wouldn't have the choices, freedoms and health we do today.

Of course, it is still on us to pioneer and embrace the changes. Some of the most basic ways to put things into perspective, is found in how we think about:

- Work
- Money
- Saving
- Investments
- Wealth
- How we choose to spend our time

Moreover, we can't just wait until something stops working to start thinking about how we can do better. It would be foolish to wait until all our fossil fuels and natural energy sources are used up before we start thinking about alternatives. It would be worse to wait to think about how we'll feed our families and keep a roof over our heads until all our savings have been vaporized. It's sad to wait until you are 90 to realize what you wanted most in life was to spend more time with your kids when they were young. It's never too late though. We'll never be as young as we are today. So, whether you've just started working a part-time job and are getting your first paycheck, are a highly paid professional with a sizable 401k, or are in retirement and still have goals, it's always wise to ask yourself, "what's next?" What can you do differently, or advance into, in order to improve things?

The Need for Constant Innovation & Improvement
We don't all have to be Alexander Graham Bell, Albert Einstein, Socrates, Da Vinci, Christopher Columbus, Steve Jobs, or Elon Musk like inventors, thinkers, and explorers. Yet, we can, and should all be seeking constant improvement in our lives. Not just for ourselves, but for others too.

This can be simple things, like tweaking your diet and workout plan. It can be your monthly budget. Or it can be in how we diversify our investments each year.

No matter what it is we want to improve on, it all starts with learning.
We can:
- Take courses
- Participate in webinars
- Watch YouTube videos
- Attend conferences
- Read books
- Find mentors
- Test out new things

What may appear to be big leaps, gains, and overnight successes are really just the culmination of these small efforts and tweaks adding up.

I've also invested many years in teaching and mentoring others. I believe that once you've learned something valuable that can also help others, you have a responsibility to share it with them too.

Balancing Disruption & Growth

From 2008 to 2016 we saw a huge surge in interest in innovation, entrepreneurship, invention, startups, and new things. 'Disruption' became the mission and motto of thousands of entrepreneurs and organizations. Many even started breaking things, just because. Sometimes that worked. In other cases it became a multiple year detour, before figuring out there were some solid reasons for the ways somethings were being done after all.

If you change things too much, people don't get it, or you end up losing foundational, timeless principles that are vital. We've definitely seen this in startup attempts in real estate and finance. There needs to be a balance between innovation for growth and improvement, and core principles.

Apple is a great example of this. It can be really annoying when Apple announces yet another new iPhone, right after you bought the latest version. Despite that, after the groundbreaking iPod and iPhone, which were huge leaps, Apple has consistently added new innovative upgrades, without dramatically changing the design of the devices. And people get it. Those who want the best features upgrade. As Seth Godin points out though, despite the fact that we no longer need traditional cars, automakers keep churning them out with the same basic features, because they are proven, and people get it. We don't actually need gas pedals, or steering wheels, or even windscreens or rear windows anymore. Cameras, an iPad screen, and an Xbox style controller, inside a more comfortable self-driving living room design would work today. Not everyone is ready for that though. So, we have hybrid cars that give the enjoyment of really driving, the ease of parking themselves, the safety of alerting you to things in your path, are better for the world, and give you the ability to move efficiently in the short term, but still go the distance.

There have been a lot of technological advances in the world of real estate and finance too. Some are great. Others not so much. We now have more powerful research and screening capabilities than ever before. We can better evaluate the market and individual assets, screen backgrounds of vendors and tenants; and all at the tip of your fingers and shareable so you can collaborate with your team on it. So much more of the business has gone paperless, has been streamlined with cloud based storage, and has become overall more efficient. That means investors can enjoy historically high profits on notes and real estate, while being more confident in making great investments. Unfortunately though, not all banks, investment houses, and funds like to share the greater spreads attainable with their investor clients.

Some of the companies that have only gotten in since 2008, have great tech ideas and have enjoyed a great short term run in the following surge. Unfortunately though, many haven't been around long enough to know how to navigate leaner times, or don't even have a plan for sustainability.

So disrupt, embrace what's new, but make sure it is built on solid principles that last.

Chapter 11:
Bonus Chapter: Can a Fund Change the World?

A fund is not just a money making vehicle.

Fueling Innovation & Thinking Bigger

Investing in a fund may just be a tool for you to make more money. Everyone needs an income to preserve, and to grow their wealth. A fund, and your individual investments have the power to do a lot more than that too, however.

For one, stepping into something which can better protect your capital, and maximize its growth, can empower you to do a whole lot more. You can enjoy the passive income produced by investing, and the time it potentially frees up for you.

We all have a duty to do the best we can, even in our investments. This could give you the free time you crave to spend with kids while they are still kids, or to spend with parents while they are still around. It could give you the time to better a relationship, or go make a positive difference in others' lives by supporting a cause you are passionate about.

Preserving capital and generating better returns could also give you the financial surplus you need to help others. That can range from being able to send your kids to college or house your aging parents, to building affordable housing in Mexico, India, or your backyard. The extra income can even be grown and turned into an endowment or trust to support cancer or Alzheimer's research and cures. The fact of the matter is that if we are not demanding the most from our investments, then we are just throwing money away for the most part, or giving it to organizations and people who are going to use it to fatten their own pockets.

The money I've made along the way is great. Yet, it has been the interaction and direct impact on individuals' and families lives', and bringing a better alternative to the market for borrowers, sellers, and investors that is truly priceless.

World Changing Funds
Funds can and do change the world.

Some funds anchor entire countries, like Norway's Sovereign Fund. It's a trillion dollar global fund that has the equivalent of $190,000 invested for each citizen. Others like Blackstone and big banking giants have altered the economies and landscapes of third world countries. At least temporarily. Fund manager Bill Ackman has tried to push new records in prices. That includes the $90M purchase of a condo in NYC (that was trumped by someone else at $100M), which he hopes to flip for $500M. Sadly though, his investments in pharma resulted in an epic scandal and $4B loss for investors after the price gouging case against "Pharma Bro."

Then there are big corporate funds and nonprofit funds, which focus on social enterprises. IBM does some work in education, for example. There is also a US Fund which supports UNICEF, and the Acumen fund which is essentially a charity that invests donor money in new startups in poor countries. And then certain funds just focus on renewable energy, to give some examples.

Unfortunately, the Norwegian pension fund has only been returning about 4%, after its massive cut in fees, according to CNN Money. Promisingly though, a Morgan Stanley report shows that sustainable investment funds focused on doing good have met or exceeded the returns of traditional funds. In fact, 72% have shown higher profitability, and lower volatility.

It's incredibly encouraging to see that you can operate and invest in an ethical organization, which both enriches the community and helps the individuals it touches, but can also produce average returns for investors.

Chapter 12:
Enhancing Strategic Thinking

In order to become successful strategic investors, we need to maximize our strategic thinking abilities.

The Most In-Demand Skill

According to Mark Cuban, creative and critical thinking will be the #1, most in demand skill in the next few years, as most tasks and functions are being taken over by technology. Also, we are piling up big masses of data. The problem is that we still need real humans who can make sense of and apply human logic to it. We have all the information coming in, but investors need to be able to decipher what it really means.

Some of us may seem to be born with more imagination and analytic thinking, but these things can be learned, and also improved on. In fact, it is so important that it deserves dedicated time. On the bright side, getting better in this area doesn't require a degree, student loans, or going back to college for four more years.

Secondary to this, Cuban says, is a demand for people who focus on having a social impact, especially in corporate America.

10 Ways to Boost Creative Thinking

Try out some of these tactics for boosting your creative thinking skills, and keep working those which work for you.

1. Exercise

Simply walking is a great way to find your "eureka!" moments. It gives you new input each day, makes you feel good, keeps both your brain and body healthy, and distracts parts of your brain, allowing you to focus on different ways of thinking. Running is great too. Or try a yoga class. Think of different exercises you can do with the same weights or machines in order to break through physical plateaus, and you'll naturally improve your creativity. The same thing goes even if you can't make it to the gym. How can you create new body weight exercises at home or on the road, or create improvised weights? If you aren't feeling very creative at first, try something like Beach Body which gives you access to a wide variety of exercise routines, from Brazilian dance moves to work your abs, to military style training, and high interval training.

2. Diet

What you eat and drink can make a significant difference in brain health. Just trying out and shopping for new foods,   and experimenting with cooking or mixing new drinks can really help spur creativity.

WebMD recommends[6]:
- Blueberries
- Wild salmon
- Almonds
- Brazil nuts
- Flax seed
- Sesame seed
- Avocadoes

---

[6] http://www.webmd.com/diet/features/eat-smart-healthier-brain#1

- Oatmeal
- Black beans
- Pomegranate juice
- Tea
- Dark chocolate

Other foods and drinks that are highly recommended include eggs, broccoli, and green tea. If you really want to take brain hacking to a new level, check out what they are doing at Bulletproof Coffee. Some even suggest alcohol can help.

3. Mix Up Your Routine
One study has shown that individuals who prepared their breakfast sandwiches in reverse order actually brainstormed more productively afterwards. Routines are good, but keep things fresh, especially when you want to get some creative thinking done. Brush your teeth, make your coffee, and get dressed in a different order. Take a different route to work, or ride your bike instead of taking an Uber. Have dessert before dinner, take the morning off to play and work later, or drive the kids to school instead of sticking them on the bus. Work from home and then go to the office for lunch or happy hour. The options are endless.

4. Listen
Music has been found to be great for creative thinking. Just listening to music in general can help. Classical music is often touted as being the solution. Other studies have shown that it is really about the music you like best. Quiet may be good for focus and detailed tasks, but ambient music is said to be ideal for creative thinking. And if music is not your thing, try podcasts, a TV documentary in the background, the ocean, or the buzz of a coffee shop.

5. Travel

There is nothing like traveling to help you gain a new perspective and find different ways to look at things. Discover different scenery, cultures, languages, words and phrases, mindsets, and ways of doing things. Hang out in different neighborhoods, other parts of your state, in different states, and explore new countries. Set some goals here. That could be one new state and one new country per year. Or it could be crammed into a yearlong trip.

6. Play Video Games

ScienceDirect research proves that playing video games improves creative thinking[7]. Swallow your pride and use this as your pass to take an hour out of the day to play Xbox with your kids. Take off to an arcade on the weekends, or go on a Pokémon Go adventure.

7. Allow Yourself to Day Dream

Lifehacker says daydreaming is one of the best ways to boost creative thinking[8]. Don't pressure or limit yourself to having to think logically or figuring something out. Let your mind just wander and wonder. We simply don't take enough time to do this. That's one of the biggest differences we may find between us and history's most famous inventors and thinkers.

8. Practice Creativity When Tired

This may not sound like your ideal time to do extra brain work,

---

[7]
http://www.sciencedirect.com/science/article/pii/S074
7563211002147?via%3Dihub
[8] http://lifehacker.com/5990617/nine-of-the-best-ways-to-boost-creative-thinking

but Fast Company names it as one of its ways to transform creative thinking[9]. Just like when exercising in a different routine, if one muscle is tired, the others are forced pitch in. The same is true with the mind. This can work in the morning, late at night, or around your afternoon naps. Famous artist Salvador Dali used to purposely rig himself to be shocked back awake if he fell asleep in his chair so that he could best harness his subconscious or 'hypnopompic' state.

9. Consume New Content

Consuming new content is one of the best ways to learn to think differently, while giving you new perspectives. If all you read is nonfiction business books, pick up a fiction book just to change it up. If you normally read meaty business blogs try out some fun list type articles or magazines. If you typically listen to podcasts, try out some YouTube content. Read up on people who have opposite views than yours. Take a trip to a museum you normally wouldn't be interested in, or go to a different type of concert.

10. Create Something Daily

Seth Godin is famous for saying the best way to accomplish something or get good at something like blogging, is just to do it every day. Do it consistently, no matter whether you are tired or uninspired, or whether you think it is good or not. It could be writing, art, sudoku, models, great tea, paper airplanes, or new relationships. Just pick something.

---

[9] https://www.fastcompany.com/3028465/10-surprising-ways-to-transform-your-creative-thinking

7 Ways to Boost Strategic Thinking

Creative thinking helps with the big picture and problem solving. It can be pivotal in seeing and achieving your full potential, while navigating challenges along the journey. Strategic thinking takes those ideas, and forms them into a tangible strategy, gives you direction, and helps you to formulate tactics and make decisions which will carry you through to your big vision and goals. While there may be some crossover, strategic thinking is the logic, which makes the creative ideas a reality.

Try these seven ways for boosting strategic thinking capabilities.

1. Practice Connecting the Dots
Speaking on his theory of great thinking, Steve Jobs says, "Creativity is just connecting things. When you ask creative people how they did something, they feel a little guilty because they didn't really do it, they just saw something." The same applies to strategic thinking. Often, the big breakthroughs and wins just come from connecting the dots in a different way than others do. There are various ways to practice this. You can brainstorm on paper or by using mind maps online. Or you can practice one of those dot and line exercises or games like these on the following pages.

Bus · Rock · burp · dull · candy · crazy · bumpy · eager · giant
Hide · mailbox · clue · Ride · back- · cheese · funny
oil · Towel · ninja · angry · girl · hot · refrigerator
Paints · window · candle · books · artist · jealous
Blend · Cut · vase · Ugly · van · kind · intelligent
Juicy · Blanket · time · Smelly · Tail · mad · lazy · playground
Icy · Kooky · Shower · swim · flag · naughty · Run
Hard · chair · Mex · Rich · apple
Hill · Large · Messy · step · Quick · 20 · 1 · Fork · phone
Gentle · 18 · 19 · 2 · drink
Foolish · lamp · 17 · button · lemonade · 3 · squeal
Nice · 16 · popcorn · skip · 4 · Baseball · bottle
Excellent · Perfect · 15 · octagonal · fairy
Guitar · snack · Old · 14 · drive · 5 · horse · jewels
Librarian · Dry · 13 · 7 · 8 · purple · school
princess · calculator · 12 · Careful · Blue · quiet · sneeze · Ruler · pencil
Banana · write · 11 · 9 · Above · round · hamburger · juggle · ostrich · Paint
keys · zesty · young · Camera · jump · bubble · water
Stove · Cereal · shoes · 10 · weak · silly · look · doctor
chocolate · scissors · Popsicle · venomous · X · tasty · Grapes · Music
Exercise · snap · unique
ring

105

Stretching Your Thinking
The Nine Dot Exercise
Connect all dots with only 4 straight lines and without lifting your pen

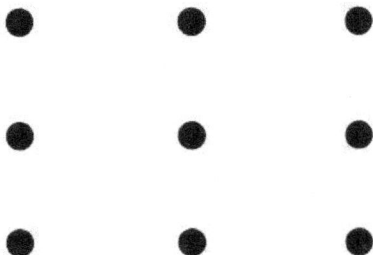

●   ●   ●

●   ●   ●

●   ●   ●

2. Talk it Out

Sometimes the best way to develop and refine your strategy is to talk it out. Get it out of your head and into real words. Just speaking it out loud to someone else can sometimes help you answer your own questions. You might just need a good listener after all. It can also help to get feedback, as we mentioned above. One of the great things about having a partner in business and life is having someone to bounce ideas back and forth with. Online forums can work too. Just be objective when weighing the feedback you get.

3. Play Strategy Games

Chess, backgammon, Go, Chinese checkers, and Risk are all classic strategy games. Play them in person or play them online. Test yourself against AI or various new opponents. This is a great way to connect and surround yourself with other strategic thinkers and smart minds. As they say, "iron sharpens iron."

4. Practice Martial Arts

Martial arts are a fantastic way to develop the mind and your strategic thinking. It's not really all about force and hurting people. In fact, it can be quite the opposite. Brazilian Jiu Jitsu is very strategic. You have to learn to think steps ahead to avoid being caught in a hold, and to know how to be able to get out of one. Real world self-defense classes can teach you how to look for escape routes and improvise weapons or tools to defend yourself with in everyday objects. Tae Kwon Do teaches you how to look for new strategies to score points on your opponent. Try out different styles to develop a healthy body, mind and agility in strategic thinking.

5. Brain Game Apps

Nowadays, there are a variety of apps you can install on your phone so that you can fit in a few minutes of brain training and stay productive during any downtime. Lumosity is probably the most famous. It even lets you test and rank against others. Elevate, Peak, Fit Brains and Cognifit are all recommended by Medical News Today[10]. Have at least one of these on your phone.

6. Mental Exercises

You can have a lot of fun with this one. You can do it alone, play it with family, or use it as an icebreaker. Ask questions like "Would you rather ___ or _____?" or "What would you do if..." It will get you thinking, help create new links in your brain and develop our natural ability to strategize and solve issues fast. What if you

---

[10] http://www.medicalnewstoday.com/articles/316684.php

were kidnapped, right now, from where you are, and were thrown in the trunk of a vehicle? What would you do? Would you rather win the lottery today, knowing that you would lose it all within 24 hours, or invest 30% of everything you have, and know you'll be a multi-millionaire in 20 years?

7. Hire for it
We don't have to do it all alone. If you don't have a strong strategic partner or accountability group, hire some help. Hire a strategist, get a coach, bring in an on-demand consultant, or give your current advisors, accountants, and assistants more leeway, and encourage them to bring you better ideas.

Designing Your Thinking Space
Clearly, some of the above creative and strategic thinking practices, exercises, and experiments can be done anywhere. Others can be done in your own special thinking space. Do you have one?

Where do you do most of your thinking? Where do you think best? Is it at the beach, in your hot tub, on your balcony, in your office, or somewhere else? Finding and designing the best thinking space for you can make a world of difference.

I block two thinking periods per week. One is at my home office. And the other is at a local Korean heat therapy spa. This type of heat therapy has been used since the times of the ancient Greek and Roman Empires, and has many physical benefits. Some of these include making you feel great, and facilitating better thinking. Cold therapy is highly raved about too. Many leading minds, like Tony Robbins, have gone as far as getting cryotherapy chambers installed at home.

While there are certainly benefits in collaboration, I like to do most of my thinking where I have peace and quiet. Despite recent trends in open flow plan offices and coworking spaces, Harvard Business Review says this "may be too much of a good thing," adding that people are "rediscovering the value of quiet and focus in spaces where they can concentrate[11].

It really comes down to what works best for you. You can try busy cluttered spaces that may give your mind more fuel, or clean slate minimalist spaces that are less distracting. Try standing desks, or comfortable seating. Try tight spaces for concentration, or open space with wall sized whiteboards that let you move around passionately. You'll want to be able to have some control over noise, temperature, and lighting, if you want to completely optimize your space and be at your peak. Color makes a difference too. According to a health blog, blue is the optimal color for boosting creative thinking[12]. Green is a good runner up. Red is supposed to be ideal for focused tasks and concentration. Some may feel more awake with bright lighting, while others say they work better with softer lighting. A great way to streamline your testing is to use smart lighting. New smart lights like Philips' Hue can enable you to change the color, warmth, and brightness of a room just by using special light bulbs. Use them to transform your space depending on the task or type of thinking at hand.

Scheduling Time to Think

We must schedule time to think, and defend it vigorously. People will hijack your time. Marketers are doing it every moment of the

---

[11] https://hbr.org/2016/05/7-factors-of-great-office-design
[12] https://www.ahealthblog.com/10-proven-ways-to-help-boost-creative-thinking.html /

day. Even your own team, family, and friends will hijack your time. They don't mean to do it, but in order to help them to the best of your ability, you must defend your time firmly.

I put myself "on vacation," when I need to create time to think or focus on the most important and profitable tasks in my business. I'm away 'on vacation,' even to my in-house team at the office at times. I'll work from home, and only go into the office when I need to. I also personally schedule 3 hours 2 times a week just for thinking as detailed above.

Block your time in advance, disconnect, and find your sweet spot for getting your strategic thinking done. If you need to, create a voicemail greeting and email autoresponder that tells everyone you are away so they don't get frustrated, and your precious time isn't compromised.

The twice a week ritual works for me, but find what is right for you. It may be a daily routine, a monthly day out, or even an annual getaway for two weeks.

Getting Started

We've covered many factors in becoming more strategic, conscious, purposeful, and successful investors. I've shared some of my journey, and trust you've found some value in the lessons I learned along the way. We talked about laying out a game plan, enhancing strategic thinking, and having the right mindset.

We've also dug into different asset classes, laid out the truth about real estate, talked about the various forms of financial and property investments - and how these can all be weaved together in a hybrid approach to achieve great results now, and sustainable results for the future.

We even touched on how you can pursue this strategy yourself, and maybe even build your own fund, or develop this approach into a new line to introduce your investment clients to.

Of course, I'd love for you to check out the fund to see if it is a good fit for you. More importantly though, I want you to pursue what you find fantastically motivating, what drives you, fills you with happiness, and sets you free. I want you to live out your full potential. And investing is key to achieving that.

So, keep learning, commit yourself to invest, and do so as best as you can. Look for investments that not only generate great returns, but that don't do any harm out there either, and you may find that you can achieve far more than you dreamed.

References:

https://www.allbusiness.com/top-10-reasons-to-invest-money-93916-1.html

http://www.remodeling.hw.net/cost-vs-value/2017/

http://www.calculatedriskblog.com/2012/12/lawler-on-upward-trend-in-real-house.html

http://money.cnn.com/2017/09/19/investing/norway-pension-fund-trillion-dollars/index.html

http://www.causeartist.com/changing-the-world-through-social-impact-investing/